Presenting an Effective
and Dynamic Technical Paper

Dedication

To the two women in my life who helped me with this book: my wife June whose persistent encouragement pushed me to get it finished and who provided many useful comments on its organization and content, and my daughter Brigette who designed the cover and created all the illustrations that reinforce the content of this book and make it more enjoyable to read.

Presenting an Effective and Dynamic Technical Paper
A Guidebook for Novice and Experienced Speakers in a Multicultural World

William B. Krantz
Professor Emeritus and President's Teaching Scholar,
University of Colorado, Boulder, CO, United States

Professor Emeritus and Ohio Eminent Scholar,
University of Cincinnati, Cincinnati, OH, United States

AMSTERDAM • BOSTON • HEIDELBERG • LONDON
NEW YORK • OXFORD • PARIS • SAN DIEGO
SAN FRANCISCO • SINGAPORE • SYDNEY • TOKYO
Academic Press is an imprint of Elsevier

Academic Press is an imprint of Elsevier
125 London Wall, London EC2Y 5AS, United Kingdom
525 B Street, Suite 1800, San Diego, CA 92101-4495, United States
50 Hampshire Street, 5th Floor, Cambridge, MA 02139, United States
The Boulevard, Langford Lane, Kidlington, Oxford OX5 1GB, United Kingdom

Copyright © 2017 Elsevier Inc. All rights reserved.

No part of this publication may be reproduced or transmitted in any form or by any means, electronic or mechanical, including photocopying, recording, or any information storage and retrieval system, without permission in writing from the publisher. Details on how to seek permission, further information about the Publisher's permissions policies and our arrangements with organizations such as the Copyright Clearance Center and the Copyright Licensing Agency, can be found at our website: www.elsevier.com/permissions.

This book and the individual contributions contained in it are protected under copyright by the Publisher (other than as may be noted herein).

Notices
Knowledge and best practice in this field are constantly changing. As new research and experience broaden our understanding, changes in research methods, professional practices, or medical treatment may become necessary.

Practitioners and researchers must always rely on their own experience and knowledge in evaluating and using any information, methods, compounds, or experiments described herein. In using such information or methods they should be mindful of their own safety and the safety of others, including parties for whom they have a professional responsibility.

To the fullest extent of the law, neither the Publisher nor the authors, contributors, or editors, assume any liability for any injury and/or damage to persons or property as a matter of products liability, negligence or otherwise, or from any use or operation of any methods, products, instructions, or ideas contained in the material herein.

British Library Cataloguing-in-Publication Data
A catalogue record for this book is available from the British Library

Library of Congress Cataloging-in-Publication Data
A catalog record for this book is available from the Library of Congress

ISBN: 978-0-12-805418-5

For Information on all Academic Press publications
visit our website at https://www.elsevier.com

Publisher: Sara Tenney
Acquisition Editor: Mary Preap
Editorial Project Manager: Joslyn Chaiprasert-Paguio
Production Project Manager: Edward Taylor
Designer: Mark Rogers

Typeset by MPS Limited, Chennai, India

Transferred to Digital Printing in 2017

Glossophobia or speech anxiety is the fear of public speaking or of speaking in general. The word comes from the Greek γλῶσσα *glōssa*, meaning tongue, and φόβος *phobos*, fear or dread.

Wikipedia, the free encyclopedia (https://en.wikipedia.org/)

science & technology books

ELSEVIER

Companion Web Site:

http://booksite.elsevier.com/9780128054185

Presenting an Effective and Dynamic Technical Paper
William B. Krantz

TOOLS FOR ALL YOUR TEACHING NEEDS
textbooks.elsevier.com

ACADEMIC PRESS

To adopt this book for course use, visit http://textbooks.elsevier.com.

Contents

Preface		xi
Acknowledgments		xv
Testimonials From Student Award Winners		xvii

1. Introduction ... 1

    1.1 Focus and Scope of This Guidebook ... 1
    1.2 Formal Oral Versus Poster Presentations ... 3
    1.3 Special Features of This Guidebook ... 3
    1.4 How to Use This Guidebook ... 4

2. Preliminary Considerations ... 7

    2.1 Focus and Scope of This Chapter ... 7
    2.2 The Presentation Format ... 8
    2.3 The Venue ... 8
    2.4 The Allotted Time ... 9
    2.5 The Outline and Cue Cards for Your Presentation ... 9
        2.5.1 Importance of Preparing an Outline ... 9
        2.5.2 Value of Preparing Cue Cards ... 10
    2.6 Dressing for the Occasion ... 11

3. Organizing Your Presentation ... 15

    3.1 Focus and Scope of This Chapter ... 15
    3.2 The Abstract ... 16
        3.2.1 When an Abstract Is Needed ... 16
        3.2.2 Content of an Abstract ... 16
    3.3 The Title Slide ... 17
        3.3.1 What It Must Include ... 17
        3.3.2 What Else It Can Include ... 18
    3.4 The Outline or Overview ... 18
    3.5 The Introduction ... 19
    3.6 The Review of Prior Studies ... 19
    3.7 The Research Plan ... 19
        3.7.1 Indicating the Design Considerations ... 19
        3.7.2 Indicating How the Problem Will be Addressed ... 20
        3.7.3 Research Plan for an Experimental Study ... 20
        3.7.4 Research Plan for a Theoretical Development ... 21

	3.8	The Discussion of Results	22
		3.8.1 Showing Typical Results	22
		3.8.2 Presenting Your Results	22
		3.8.3 Providing Some Measure of Reproducibility	22
		3.8.4 Emphasizing Interesting Observations	23
	3.9	The Conclusions	23
	3.10	A Future Work Slide	24
	3.11	The Acknowledgments	24
	3.12	The "Thank You" Slide	24
4.	**Making a Formal Oral Presentation**		**27**
	4.1	Focus and Scope of This Chapter	27
		4.1.1 Importance of an Effective Presentation Style	27
		4.1.2 Distinguishing Features of Making a Formal Oral Presentation	27
		4.1.3 Developing Your Own Presentation Style	28
	4.2	Preparing Your Slides	28
		4.2.1 Preliminary Considerations in Preparing Your Slides	28
		4.2.2 Making Your Visuals Easy to Understand	29
		4.2.3 Choosing an Appropriate Font	29
		4.2.4 Choosing an Appropriate Font Size	30
		4.2.5 Choosing an Appropriate Color Scheme	30
		4.2.6 Emphasizing Important Parts of Your Presentation	31
		4.2.7 Use of Animations and Sounds	32
		4.2.8 Choosing a Template	32
		4.2.9 Numbering Your Slides	32
		4.2.10 Proofreading Your Presentation	33
	4.3	Scoping Out the Room and Facilities When On-Site	33
		4.3.1 Scoping Out the Room for Your Presentation	33
		4.3.2 Scoping Out the Facilities for Your Presentation	34
	4.4	Use of a Microphone and Laser Pointer	35
		4.4.1 Use of a Microphone	35
		4.4.2 Use of a Laser Pointer	35
	4.5	Mastering the Mechanics of an Effective Oral Presentation	36
		4.5.1 Your Appearance	36
		4.5.2 Vocalization	36
		4.5.3 Effective Eye Contact	38
		4.5.4 Body Language	40
		4.5.5 Use of Humor	40
		4.5.6 Handling a Momentary Lapse-of-Memory	41
	4.6	Stepping Through Your Presentation	42
		4.6.1 Your Introduction by the Session Chair or Host	43
		4.6.2 Generating Interest Early in Your Presentation	43
		4.6.3 Pacing Your Presentation	45
		4.6.4 Ending Your Presentation	46
		4.6.5 Handling Questions Including Those You Cannot Answer	47
	4.7	Handling Nervousness	48
		4.7.1 Channeling Nervousness Into Projecting Excitement	48

		4.7.2	Ways to Control Nervousness	49
		4.7.3	Handling Mistakes That Cause Nervousness	49
		4.7.4	The Easiest Way to Avoid Nervousness	50
	4.8	Practice Makes Perfect		50
	4.9	Critiquing Presentations Made by Others		51
	4.10	Developing Your Presentation Style		51

5. Giving a Poster Presentation — 53

- 5.1 Focus and Scope of This Chapter — 53
  - 5.1.1 Distinguishing Features of a Poster Presentation — 53
  - 5.1.2 Importance of Developing Your Own Poster Presentation Style — 54
- 5.2 Preparing Your Poster — 55
  - 5.2.1 The Plan for Laying Out Your Poster — 55
  - 5.2.2 Organizing the Content of Your Poster — 55
  - 5.2.3 Designing Your Poster — 56
  - 5.2.4 Proofreading Your Poster Material — 57
- 5.3 Printing Your Poster — 57
  - 5.3.1 Choices in the Format for Printing Your Poster — 57
  - 5.3.2 Proofreading Your Printed Poster — 59
- 5.4 Checklist Before Arriving On-Site for Your Poster Presentation — 60
- 5.5 Scoping Out the Room and Posting Your Poster — 60
  - 5.5.1 Scoping Out the Room for Your Poster Presentation — 60
  - 5.5.2 Posting Your Poster — 61
- 5.6 Using a Mechanical Pointer — 61
  - 5.6.1 Use a Mechanical Pointer for a Poster Presentation — 61
  - 5.6.2 Using a Mechanical Pointer to Control Your Audience — 62
  - 5.6.3 Avoid "Playing" With Your Mechanical Pointer — 62
- 5.7 Mastering the Mechanics of an Effective Poster Presentation — 63
  - 5.7.1 Preliminary Considerations — 63
  - 5.7.2 Engaging Your Audience — 63
  - 5.7.3 Interacting With Your Audience — 63
  - 5.7.4 "Gimmicks" for Making an Effective Poster Presentation — 64
- 5.8 Poster Session Courtesy — 65
  - 5.8.1 Courtesy Considerations for Poster Presentations — 65
  - 5.8.2 Courtesy Considerations Regarding Your Audience — 65
  - 5.8.3 Courtesy Considerations Regarding Other Poster Presenters — 67
- 5.9 Developing Your Poster Presentation Style — 67

Appendix A: Quick Reference Guide for Giving a Formal Oral Presentation — 69
Appendix B: Quick Reference Guide for Making a Poster Presentation — 71
Appendix C: Typical Criteria for Judging a Poster Competition — 73
Appendix D: Considerations When Critiquing a Presentation — 75
Appendix E: Web Sites for Outstanding Presentations — 79
Appendix F: Overview of Online Materials — 85
Index — 89

Preface

There are always three speeches, for every one you actually gave. The one you practiced, the one you gave ... and the one you wish you gave!
Dale Carnegie, American developer of courses in public speaking, and interpersonal skills.

The author's interest in public speaking skills was sparked by his English teacher in high school who had the students in his class give short speeches. The teacher was sufficiently impressed with the author's speaking ability that he encouraged him to continue his studies at a college or university. This good advice was a "game changer" for the author since at the time he had no intention of continuing his formal education. As a result in 1957 he enrolled at Saint Joseph's College in Indiana, a small liberal arts college, where he intended to major in journalism. However, he was discouraged from pursuing this major by the chair for the journalism program because the author's English grammar was so poor. This came as a bit of a shock to the author who then decided to major in chemistry, but also to improve his English. Perhaps this instilled some empathy in him for students whose first language is not English and thus who struggle with learning proper English grammar. The author proceeded to read the *Writer's Guide and Index to English*[1] cover-to-cover. Moreover, the author took every opportunity to improve his public-speaking skills. At the time it was a requirement to take a one-semester course in speech. However, the author enjoyed this course so much he elected to take the subsequent course in public speaking. He became very much interested in the power of the spoken word. Oratory competitions at the time were popular. The author entered and won a few awards for his public speaking at these competitions.

The author received a BA degree in chemistry in 1961 and pursued a BS in chemical engineering at the University of Illinois at Urbana-Champaign, which he received in 1962. He did very well in his studies at Illinois such that he was able to pursue postgraduate studies in chemical engineering at the University of California at Berkeley. Both the University of Illinois and the University of California at Berkeley had many gifted scientists and

---

1. Porter G. Perrin, *Writer's Guide and Index to English*, Scott Foresman and Company, Glenview, Illinois 1959.

engineers including a few Nobel laureates on their faculties. The author observed that many of these faculty were not so gifted in presenting their research work in lectures and seminars. In some cases it seemed that the distinguished scientist or engineer somehow thought that the excellence of their research was sufficient to ensure effective communication to the audience.

Another observation made by the author during his college and university studies was that the curriculum for students studying in the sciences and engineering was so packed with technical courses that it did not provide much opportunity for them to develop their communication skills. In fact, at the time graduate students at major universities such as Illinois and Berkeley did not have the opportunity to present their research work at national and international meetings. In most cases the accepted policy was that the student's work would be presented at technical meetings by their research advisor. Indeed the author never had an opportunity to make either a formal oral presentation or give a poster at any technical meetings during his 5 years of PhD studies at Berkeley. This made the author very committed to providing speaking opportunities for his students when he received his PhD in 1968 and joined the faculty in the Department of Chemical Engineering at the University of Colorado at Boulder.

It was a different day and age when the author began his academic career at Colorado. The author's department chair told him first to become a good teacher and then worry about developing a research program. Accepting such advice today would be suicidal for a young faculty member at a major research university. However, the author did follow the good advice given to him and became a very good teacher. He received many awards for teaching excellence and in particular a lifetime appointment as a President's Teaching Scholar of the University of Colorado. In this capacity he accepted an invitation to coordinate a program to help faculty improve their teaching skills by having one or more of their lectures video-recorded after which the author would provide constructive input for them. Hence, the author became a "teacher of teachers" thereby contributing to an effort to improve the lecturing skills of university educators.

The author also was committed to improving the public-speaking skills of his students. He encouraged his students to enter technical papers competitions and coached them on how to deliver an effective technical presentation. His students were extraordinarily successful in winning awards in regional and national technical papers competitions sponsored by organizations such as the American Association for the Advancement of Science, the American Institute of Chemical Engineers, the American Chemical Society, and the North American Membrane Society. Over a period of 32 years his students won 39 awards including 17 First Place awards at these competitions. It is noteworthy that 15 of these awards in technical papers competitions went to students whose first language was not English! The experience that the author gained in working with his students in preparing for these competitions laid the foundation for writing this book on "Presenting an Effective and Dynamic Technical Paper − A Guidebook for Novice and Experienced Speakers in a Multicultural World". In particular, he gained experience in coaching students whose first language was not English to not only present papers well, but also to win prestigious awards in technical papers competitions!

The author also was instrumental in creating a forum for students to gain experience in presenting talks on their research work. He was the co-founder and served for 15 years as the Co-Director of the National Science Foundation (NSF) Industry/University Cooperative Research Center (I/U CRC) for Membrane Applied Science and Technology (MAST) sites at both the University of Colorado and the University of Cincinnati. The students who worked on MAST Center research projects were required to make two oral and two poster presentations each year that were critically reviewed by the industry sponsors who provided the funding for their projects. Whereas this provided invaluable experience for the students, it also helped the author hone his skills in preparing students for both formal oral presentations and giving posters on their research work. It was also particularly helpful in gaining experience to help students make technical presentations that would be well-received by the representatives from the industry sponsors of the MAST center.

In 2005, the author retired from a full-time academic appointment and accepted a part-time faculty position in the Department of Chemical and Biomolecular Engineering at the National University of Singapore (NUS). One of the requirements at NUS was that all the PhD students take a workshop on Oral Communication Skills. This workshop was taught on a voluntary basis by one of the faculty. At the time the author joined the faculty at NUS, the Department Head was desperately looking for a faculty member to volunteer for teaching this workshop. This provided the author with a wonderful opportunity for pulling together the materials on oral communication skills that he had been developing over many years into an organized workshop. It also provided a meaningful experience to sensitize him to the multicultural aspects of public speaking, since nearly all of his students were from Asia, India, and the Middle East. The author then proceeded to offer this workshop at NUS on a regular basis.

In 2008, the author accepted an appointment as a Visiting Professor at Nanyang Technological University (NTU) in Singapore in order to help establish the Singapore Membrane Technology Center (SMTC). He subsequently was invited to offer his workshop on Oral Communications Skills for the PhD students in the SMTC that subsequently was extended to include all the PhD students in the Nanyang Environment and Water Research Institute (NEWRI) at NTU.

The author also has offered his Oral Communications Skills workshop as an invited speaker at several universities around the world. After each offering of the workshop the participating students submitted an anonymous evaluation of its effectiveness. Several students suggested that the author pull together the workshop materials into some type of a speaker's guidebook that could be used as a convenient reference when the need to prepare a presentation arose. This constructive suggestion from the workshop students led to writing this guidebook.

The Oral Communications Workshop involved two half-days of lectures in which the author discussed the organization and delivery of both a formal oral presentation and giving a poster. At the end of the first lecture the author gave an example of a formal oral presentation in which he would interrupt himself to point out how the presentation incorporated various elements of style and delivery that were discussed in the lecture. At the end of the second lecture the author gave a poster in which he challenged the students to make it difficult for him so that he could indicate how one always remains attentive to the audience. The workshop ended with each student being digitally recorded while giving a 10-minute technical presentation followed by 5 minutes of questions from the audience that consisted of the other workshop students. The workshop students also would anonymously critique the presentations of their peers using a template provided by the author. These critiques would be given to the presenter after their talk. The author then would schedule a 30-minute one-on-one consultation with each student to provide them with constructive comments on how to improve their oral communication skills. Obviously some elements of the Oral Communication Skills Workshop could not be included in this guidebook. However, the online materials available with this guidebook include a digital recording of the author giving a formal oral presentation using slides prepared with PowerPoint during which the author pauses occasionally to point out how he used the various elements of giving an effective talk. It also includes a digital recording of the author giving a poster in which he also points out how he uses the techniques discussed in this guidebook to maintain effective communication with his audience.

Reading through this guidebook will not automatically make the reader a better speaker. However, hopefully it will sensitize the reader to the elements of organizing a technical presentation and to components of an effective delivery style. Perhaps the most important message in this guidebook is that public speaking is an expression of your unique personality. You already have made a conscientious effort to improve your public speaking by obtaining a copy of this guidebook. Your public speaking ability will continue to develop over the years such that it will become an integral part of who you are. This is what makes listening to good speakers so enjoyable—each of us can "bring to the table" a very personalized way of presenting our material!

The author welcomes any feedback on the material in this guidebook and suggestions for improving it. The author can be contacted via email at krantz@colorado.edu.

Acknowledgments

Light travels faster than sound. That's why certain people appear bright until you hear them speak!
—Albert Einstein, 1921 Nobel Laureate in Physics

The author must begin by acknowledging the late Dom Wulstan Mork, his high school English teacher who encouraged him to develop his public-speaking ability and to continue his formal education. The author continued to benefit from good advice under the mentorship of Brother John Marling at Saint Joseph's College in Indiana who helped him in many ways and in particular encouraged him to enter oratory competitions.

The President's Teaching Scholars (PTS) program under the direction of Dr. Mary Ann Shea at the University of Colorado provided a wonderful opportunity for the author to learn from other excellent teachers. The PTS program through its Faculty Teaching Excellence program gave the author an opportunity to work with faculty to improve their lecturing skills.

Professor Raj Rajagopalan, former Head of the Department of Chemical and Biomolecular Engineering at the National University of Singapore, created the opportunity for the author to develop his workshop on Oral Communication Skills that helped him to develop the materials in this guidebook. A special acknowledgment is accorded to Professor Tony Fane, the founding Director of the Singapore Membrane Technology Center (SMTC), and to Professor Wang Rong, the current Director of the SMTC, who encouraged the author to offer the Oral Communications Skills Workshop on a regular basis in the SMTC.

The author would be remiss if he did not acknowledge the many students he mentored in public speaking at the University of Colorado who had the courage to enter and do so well in regional and national technical papers competitions. The author also gratefully acknowledges the many students who took his workshop on Oral Communication Skills and provided useful feedback both to improve the workshop materials and to write this guidebook.

The author also gratefully acknowledges his daughter, Brigette Elise Krantz, who created the illustrations for this guidebook. Perhaps her artwork will convince some readers that a bit of humor can make communicating both the written and spoken word more effective! He also thanks his wife,

June Clair Krantz, who encouraged him to write this book and continually prodded him to finish writing it! She also proofread all the material and contributed many helpful suggestions for making this guidebook more useful.

Finally, the author would like to acknowledge the staff of his publisher, Elsevier. The directives provided by the Elsevier staff made preparing this book much easier. In particular, the author acknowledges Joslyn T. Chaiprasert-Paguio, Editorial Project Manager, and Mary Preap, Senior Acquisitions Editor, with whom he worked closely in preparing this manuscript for publication.

Testimonials From Student Award Winners

The author has mentored students from many different countries both through his workshops on oral communication skills and working with them individually. More than 50 of these students have won major awards in formal oral and poster technical papers competitions. In particular, the author has helped many students whose first language was not English win awards in technical papers competitions. The following student testimonials attest to the effectiveness of the public-speaking techniques advanced in this guidebook.

Dr. Sim Siang Tze Victor from Singapore won First Place Awards at two international technical papers competitions during his PhD studies at Nanyang Technological University:

> *My sincere appreciation goes out to my mentor, Professor Dr. William B. Krantz for his inspirational advice and critiques. Without his valuable inputs, a number of my awards would not have been possible. In particular, I have him to thank for the Young Leaders Award at the International Desalination Association (IDA) World Congress 2011 and the Patron Prize at the 8th International Membrane Science and Technology Conference (IMSTEC) 2013 for the best oral presentations I have been awarded. It has been my utmost pleasure to be under your tutelage.*

Dr. Sim Siang Tze Victor (left) from Singapore receiving one of several awards he won.

xviii Testimonials From Student Award Winners

Jian-Yuan Lee from Malaysia won the Best Paper Award at the 2015 European Membrane Society Meeting in Aachen Germany and a Best Poster Award at the 2016 Singapore International Water Week (SIWW) Conference during his PhD studies at Nanyang Technological University:

My poster has been selected as one of the Best Student Posters of SIWW 2016! Thank you very much for your help and support during the preparation of this poster and I really appreciate it!

Zhao Jie from China won the Best Student Poster Award at the 10th Aseanian (Association of Southeast Asian Nations) Membrane Society Conference in 2016 in Nara Japan during his PhD studies at Nanyang Technological University:

I would like to express my sincere thanks to you for your very useful instructions on oral communication. I tried to follow all your tips such as mechanical pointer, name cards box and small free-take posters. Thank you very much again.

Zhao Jie from China giving his poster at the 10th Aseanian Membrane Society Conference.

Dr. Siew-Leng Loo from Malaysia won First Place in the Student Poster Competition at the Conference on "Engineering With Membranes 2013: Towards a Sustainable Future" in 2013 in Saint-Pierre d'Oléron France during her PhD studies at Nanyang Technological University:

Thank you for delivering such an informative workshop on oral communication. The workshop has given me a comprehensive picture of what to expect when presenting. This information has been a useful guide to me on the preparations that need to be made in advance. In addition, your tips on how to effectively channel nervousness into enthusiasm have been particularly helpful to me. Thanks again for helping me to overcome my fear of public speaking!

Chapter 1

Introduction

According to most studies, people's number one fear is public speaking. Number two is death! Does that sound right? This means to the average person, if you go to a funeral, you're better off in the casket than doing the eulogy!

—Jerry Seinfeld, American comedian and producer

1.1 FOCUS AND SCOPE OF THIS GUIDEBOOK

This guidebook is intended for both experienced speakers as well as those aspiring to improve their communication skills in making a presentation on a technical subject. Although this guidebook focuses on giving a technical presentation, some sections, particularly the material in Chapter 4, Making a Formal Oral Presentation, that discusses presentation delivery style, will be of value even when giving a talk on a nontechnical subject.

The focus of any technical presentation is to communicate the results of scientific inquiry, research, and technical development. In general, a technical talk should motivate the audience via an effective introduction that underscores the importance of the focus area and identifies the technical challenges. In most technical talks it is appropriate to provide a brief review of prior studies on the particular subject. This should lead to well-defined objectives of the technical work. The approach to addressing the technical challenges needs to be clearly summarized. The results of the study must be given in a form appropriate to the subject. They then need to be discussed and lead to relevant conclusions. This guidebook will provide a template for organizing a technical talk that will include a discussion of various effective ways to develop each part of a presentation.

2 Presenting an Effective and Dynamic Technical Paper

There are three things to aim at in public speaking: first, to get into your subject, then to get your subject into yourself, and lastly, to get your subject into the heart of your audience.

—Alexander Gregg, clergyman (1819–93)

The multicultural focus of this guidebook relates both to the audience and to the speaker. It includes considerations such as how to list the names of the coauthors on your presentation as well as to how to handle eye contact and use humor. These and other factors can differ across the spectrum of world cultures. Since English is often the default language at international conferences and symposia, speakers for whom English is not their first language sometimes face special concerns that will be addressed in this guidebook. Moreover, this guidebook will help speakers making a presentation in a country having a different culture than their own.

The reader should view this guidebook as a means to develop their own unique presentation style. The author does not intend this guidebook to be a series of dictates that must be followed in making a presentation. Rather the intent is to provide a possible template for organizing a talk and to give suggestions to help you develop your presentation style. Public speaking is an art in the same vein as the performing or visual arts. Just as each accomplished musician or artist can lend their own interpretation to a composition, each speaker can deliver a presentation that reflects their personality every bit as much as the way they dress or the things they enjoy in life.

1.2 FORMAL ORAL VERSUS POSTER PRESENTATIONS

Chapter 2, Preliminary Considerations, provides an overview of things you need to consider well in advance of giving your presentation. The first consideration is whether you will be giving a formal oral presentation or a poster presentation, which is usually more informal. In a formal oral presentation you are standing in front of an audience, perhaps at a podium, and have a captive audience. Typical formal presentations include papers presented in technical sessions at conferences and symposia, seminars given at a university, research institute, or company, thesis defenses, and in some job interviews and technical papers competitions. In most formal presentations you give your talk without any interruptions for questions or discussion. However, in some thesis defenses and frequently in presentations made in connection with job interviews, you will be interrupted with questions that can make giving the presentation more challenging.

Poster presentations at conferences, symposia and casual research group seminars, and some technical papers competitions tend to be more informal. Your listeners might come and go depending on their level of interest in your topic and presentation. You can expect to be interrupted for questions and even extended discussion during an informal presentation. For this reason giving an informal presentation such as a poster can be considerably more challenging than a formal oral technical talk.

The major components of both formal oral and poster presentations are organization and delivery style. The organization for both formal oral talks and poster presentations is similar and is discussed in Chapter 3, Organizing Your Presentation. However, the delivery style for a formal oral talk is quite different from that for a poster. Giving a formal oral talk is discussed in Chapter 4, Making a Formal Oral Presentation, and making a poster presentation is discussed in Chapter 5, Giving a Poster Presentation.

1.3 SPECIAL FEATURES OF THIS GUIDEBOOK

Particularly useful features of this guidebook are Appendices A and B that are Quick Reference Guides for giving either a formal oral talk or a poster presentation. For students interested in participating in technical papers competitions, Appendix C summarizes typical criteria used in judging these events. Appendix D is a worksheet developed by the author for critiquing a presentation made by someone else, which is a very good way to improve one's communications skills. Appendix E gives links to presentations made by four exceptional speakers along with a commentary on them by the author. Since this guidebook also provides access to online materials,

4   Presenting an Effective and Dynamic Technical Paper

Appendix F gives a summary and link to these materials. These include a digital recording of the author giving a PowerPoint presentation during which he periodically interrupts himself to point out how he is using the various techniques discussed in this guidebook. It also includes a digital recording of the author making a poster presentation for which the students were challenged to make it as difficult as possible for him! Different formats that can be used for laying out a poster are also included in the online materials.

1.4   HOW TO USE THIS GUIDEBOOK

After familiarizing yourself with this guidebook, it probably will be sufficient just to refresh your memory on parts of the chapters that are relevant to preparing your presentation. However, it is strongly recommended that you review the appropriate Quick Reference Guides in Appendices A and B prior to preparing and immediately before making a presentation. If your presentation is entered in a technical papers competition, it is helpful to read through the overview of typical criteria used in judging these competitions that are given in Appendix C.

I'm always trying to turn things upside down and see if they look any better.
—Tibor Kalman, American graphic designer

The comprehensive Index at the back of this guidebook is helpful to find information on any specific aspect of preparing or giving a presentation. This Index provides a convenient complement to the Quick Reference Guides in Appendices A and B.

NOTES

6 Presenting an Effective and Dynamic Technical Paper

Chapter 2

Preliminary Considerations

The P^6 Power Rule: "Proper Planning and Preparation Prevents Poor Performance!"

Stephen Keague, *The Little Red Handbook of Public Speaking and Presenting*, ISBN-10: 1470039001, ISBN-13: 978-1470039004, Ebook, 2012.

2.1 FOCUS AND SCOPE OF THIS CHAPTER

The focus of this chapter is on what you need to consider well in advance of the date for your presentation as well as immediately prior to making it. These considerations include the format, venue, and allocated time for your presentation, as well as preparing an outline and dressing appropriately for the occasion. More details are given in the subsequent chapters.

By failing to prepare, you are preparing to fail!
—Benjamin Franklin, one of the Founding Fathers of the United States

8 Presenting an Effective and Dynamic Technical Paper

2.2 THE PRESENTATION FORMAT

The format relates to whether it will be a formal oral talk or a more informal poster or presentation to your research group. Clearly it is essential to know the format for the presentation you will be giving. This information is usually given when your paper is accepted for presentation. However, if it is not given, you need to contact the person who invited you to speak or who accepted your paper as soon as possible to determine this.

2.3 THE VENUE

The venue for your presentation refers to where it will be given. Knowing this helps you prepare and make the most effective use of your slides or poster panels. Prior knowledge of the capacity of the room, whether you will be speaking with the aid of a microphone, the kind of audio—visual equipment that will be available, and if you will be confined to standing behind a podium or free to move about are important issues that can help eliminate unpleasant surprises. Usually this information can be obtained by contacting the technical session chair or your host. In the case of a poster presentation it is critical to know how much space or how many poster boards you will be allowed. It is also important to know in advance how you will attach your poster (i.e., with tape, thumbtacks, Velcro, or other means) and whether you will need to bring the appropriate materials. Obtaining as much advance information as possible about the venue is invaluable in helping you prepare your presentation. In any event it is important that you check out the room prior to making your presentation. More will be said about this in Chapter 4, Making a Formal Oral Presentation and Chapter 5, Giving a Poster Presentation.

It has been said that some people are more afraid of public speaking than they are of sharks. I doubt that any deep ocean diver has ever suddenly shouted "Watch out - A podium!"

—Unknown author

2.4 THE ALLOTTED TIME

Be aware that the time allowed for your presentation is of critical importance. There usually is a firm time allocated for formal oral presentations. Papers submitted to technical sessions typically are allowed between 15 and 30 minutes including the time permitted for questions from the audience. Invited papers such as keynote or plenary addresses typically are allowed 30–60 minutes including the time for questions from the audience. Prior to preparing your talk it is essential that you know the allotted time, preferably broken down into that allowed for your presentation and that allowed for questions from the audience.

Be sincere, be brief, be seated.
—Franklin Roosevelt, President of the United States (1933–45)

In contrast, the time allowed for an informal presentation very well might be at your own discretion. However, allocating this discretionary time can be pivotal to giving an effective informal presentation. In particular, the time you spend going through your presentation is a critical component in giving a poster presentation. This will be discussed in detail in Chapter 5, Giving a Poster Presentation. It is particularly important when participating in a technical papers poster competition to be able to give an overview of your entire poster within just a few minutes. This might be all the time you have to impress a judge with your research results and to "set the stage" for the judge to ask you a few questions.

2.5 THE OUTLINE AND CUE CARDS FOR YOUR PRESENTATION

2.5.1 Importance of Preparing an Outline

Irrespective of whether you are giving a formal oral presentation or a poster, you have a very limited amount of time to communicate your results.

In view of this, it is absolutely essential that you put considerable effort into organizing your talk. A formal outline of your entire presentation should be prepared that includes each of the major sections of a talk discussed in Chapter 3, Organizing Your Presentation. Each major section of your outline will have one or more subdivisions that indicate how the particular section will be developed. For example, the section entitled "Introduction" in your outline might have subdivisions indicating the importance of the research area, major challenges, key prior studies, and the objectives of the particular research you will be presenting. A good outline should involve just key words, not extended narrative. It should give the logical flow of your talk from introducing the topic to the conclusions drawn from the study. Your outline should indicate exactly where particular slides or poster panels will be used in your presentation. Once you have prepared an outline of your entire talk, it is important that you prepare your presentation based on this outline. An outline is provided for the PowerPoint presentation that is included with the online materials that can be accessed in connection with this guidebook.

I will literally open my mouth not knowing what is coming out.
—Leo Kottke, acoustic guitarist

2.5.2 Value of Preparing Cue Cards

Experienced speakers probably only need a good outline to prepare and give an effective presentation. However, aspiring speakers often experience nervousness or anxiety that might cause them to forget momentarily where they are in their talk. An effective way to address this problem is to prepare cue cards based on the outline for your presentation. That is, your cue cards will contain a mini-outline of your talk. Since you want to be able to put these cue cards in a convenient pocket for quick access if you need them during your talk, you want them to be small, typically 8×13 cm (3×5 in.).

Moreover, they should be numbered and written on both sides to keep the total number of cue cards to just 3 or 4. In practicing your presentation, you might find that you have a particular problem in some part of your talk such as pronouncing a certain word or remembering some important point. You should annotate your cue cards by underlining or highlighting key words to help you address such problems. For example, you can spell out phonetically a word that you have difficulty in pronouncing. In most presentations you probably will find that you never need to refer to your cue cards. However, psychologically just knowing that you have them if needed helps to give you more confidence during your presentation! The online materials that can be accessed in connection with this guidebook also include cue cards prepared for the PowerPoint presentation.

Speakers whose first language is not English might be more comfortable preparing their outline and cue cards in their native language, even when the presentation is to be made in English. Doing this can be very helpful in generating a fluid thought flow in preparing the outline and cue cards.

2.6 DRESSING FOR THE OCCASION

Dressing appropriately for your presentation shows respect for your audience and can make a difference in getting that job or winning an award in a technical papers competition. Appropriate attire has both multicultural as well as regional considerations. Appropriate attire for men from Western cultures making a formal oral presentation is usually a suit or sport coat and tie. Women have more options in dressing for a formal oral presentation. In Western cultures women can wear a dress, slacks, or business suit for a formal oral presentation. However, in non-Western cultures appropriate dress could be the formal attire in the particular culture of the speaker. Speakers from countries in Asia, the Middle East, Africa, and others most certainly can make formal presentations at meetings anywhere in the world wearing what would constitute formal attire in their own countries. Indeed, speakers smartly dressed in attire appropriate to their countries adds an attractive dimension to international meetings!

Note that dress codes are gradually being relaxed in some Western cultures such that speakers will give formal oral presentations even wearing jeans. However, in many European, Middle Eastern, Asian, Latin American, and African cultures the dress code continues to be more formal. A word of advice to aspiring young speakers is that they should err on the side of dressing more formally, particularly if they are competing for a job or an award in a technical papers competition. Whereas the younger generation in some cultures is dressing less formally, senior industry and faculty tend to be more conservative and are inclined to expect you to dress more smartly.

An exception to the formal dress code may occur when meetings are held in places that are very hot or humid. Try to find out in advance of your presentation what the dress code is for the particular meeting. If you do not know what it is, it is better to dress up and then "dress down" if appropriate.

Clothes make the man. Naked people have little or no influence on society.
—Mark Twain, American humorist

In choosing how to dress for your presentation you need to consider that you might be required to have a microphone clipped to your attire and have some place to put the transmitter for the microphone. Since you probably will have a laser-remote pointer in one hand, you do not want to encumber your other hand with holding anything else. This will restrict the use of your hands to enhance your presentation. This usually does not present a problem for male speakers. The microphone can be clipped to their tie or the lapel of their suit jacket. The transmitter for the microphone can be clipped onto their belt or put into a pocket. However, if men dress less formally, they need to consider where to clip the microphone and put the microphone transmitter. One way to handle a clip-on microphone is to wear a lanyard to which it can be attached. It is a good idea to save a lanyard given to you for your nametag at a technical meeting to use for clipping on a microphone.

This issue of clipping on the microphone and storing the microphone transmitter can be more of a problem for women. When women choose their attire for a presentation, they need to consider where the microphone can be clipped.

It needs to be approximately 20–25 cm (8–10 in.) directly below your mouth. If a woman chooses to wear a dress for her presentation, it needs to have a bodice to which the microphone can be clipped. Pull-over sweaters present particular problems for attaching the microphone. Women's business suits as well as most blouses do not present any problems with respect to clipping on the microphone. If your attire has no provision for clipping on the microphone, as was suggested above, you can wear a lanyard around your neck to which the microphone can be attached. However, storing the microphone transmitter can present a problem for women unless their attire has a large pocket or has a belt or sash. Women from Western cultures can easily find some appropriate attire that has a pocket or belt for stashing or securing the microphone transmitter. However, this can be a problem for women in some Middle Eastern, Asian, and African cultures. This concern was brought to my attention by a young woman from India who attended one of my oral communication skills workshops. She mentioned that many Indian women like to wear a sari for a formal oral presentation, which indeed is a very beautiful and elegant attire. However, a sari has no pockets, sash, or belt to store or secure the microphone transmitter. I addressed this question to my wife who is quite accomplished at designing and sewing clothes. She mentioned that it would be easy to make a small cloth sachet attached by a sash or belt into which the microphone transmitter can be placed. If you plan well enough in advance, it might even be possible to have this sachet made from the same fabric as your ethnic attire!

When a clip-on microphone is used, the session chair, cochair, or your host will usually help you attach it. However, for a woman, having a man clip the microphone onto a blouse or suit jacket could be awkward. It could be an embarrassing moment evoking laughter from the audience. You do not want unintended laughter from the audience at the beginning of your presentation when you are undoubtedly most nervous!

NOTES

14 Presenting an Effective and Dynamic Technical Paper

Chapter 3

Organizing Your Presentation

90% of how well the talk will go is determined before the speaker steps on the platform.

—Somers White, past Director of the National Speakers Association

3.1 FOCUS AND SCOPE OF THIS CHAPTER

The organization of your presentation relates to how you put your talk together. The organizational aspects of putting together both a formal as well as a poster presentation are quite similar. There are some differences that will be pointed out when the components of a talk are discussed. The possible components in a technical presentation include the abstract, title, overview, introduction, review of prior studies, research plan, discussion of results, conclusions, future work, acknowledgments, and "Thank You" slide. Depending on the format and purpose of your talk, some of these components might be omitted. Some of them such as the title, acknowledgments, and "Thank You" might be just one slide in a formal oral talk or one panel in a poster presentation. In contrast, the research plan and discussion of results might require several slides or panels. In this chapter we will discuss each of these components in the order in which they usually would be incorporated into your talk keeping in mind that you might elect to omit one or more of them for your particular presentation.

16 Presenting an Effective and Dynamic Technical Paper

If you want me to speak for an hour, I am ready today. If you want me to speak for just a few minutes, it will take me a few weeks to prepare!

—Mark Twain, American humorist

3.2 THE ABSTRACT

3.2.1 When an Abstract Is Needed

You usually need to submit an abstract for any technical paper that you plan to present either as a formal oral presentation or as a poster. Your paper will be accepted or rejected depending on how well you prepare your abstract. Hence, it is important that we discuss the organization and content of the abstract. However, an abstract is rarely used as a slide in a formal oral talk. In contrast, you might want to include a brief abstract as one of your panels at the beginning of a poster presentation.

3.2.2 Content of an Abstract

Sometimes there will be a limit on the word count allowed when submitting your abstract for possible presentation at a technical conference or symposium. This can range from a few hundred words to a single-spaced page or more. If you elect to include an abstract as one of the panels in a poster presentation, it should be short and concise. It typically should be less than 100 words, since one panel that uses sufficiently large font to be read by your audience will not permit using too many words.

The abstract should begin with a few sentences that introduce the topic of your presentation. A logical progression should follow from general considerations to the specifics on which your talk is focused. For example, you might underscore the global need for potable water and then progress to the challenge of developing more efficient ways to desalinate seawater to produce fresh water. Specifically the technical challenges you identify should lead to the focus and objectives of the work that you will be presenting.

You then should give a brief overview of the approach that you used to address the technical problem. If some aspects of your approach are novel, highlight this. End the abstract with a summary of the major results of your study. Try to avoid vague statements such as stating that your method worked better than the prior art. Rather, give some specifics such as stating that your method resulted in reducing the specific energy consumption by 25% relative to prior practice. In order to include everything required in a comprehensive abstract while keeping within the word-count limit, you can devote at most one or two sentences to each important point.

Writing an effective abstract is challenging since you are compacting your entire presentation into a few hundred words. The effort you put into writing a good abstract will be rewarded by having your paper accepted for presentation!

3.3 THE TITLE SLIDE

The first 30 seconds and the last 30 seconds have the most impact in a presentation.

—Patricia Fripp, National Speakers Association

3.3.1 What It Must Include

The title slide should include the names of the coauthors. In preparing your title slide for a presentation for an multicultural audience, it is standard to list each coauthor beginning with their given name and ending with the surname or family name. This practice is followed in the Western World. In some parts of the Middle Eastern and Asian World the order might be reversed. That is, the surname or family name might be given first followed by the given names. Note that in many parts of the Western World people have two or more given names. Standard practice is to write out only the first given name and to use the first initial of each of the other given names. Note that some people elect to use their second given name in preference to their first. In this case one uses an initial for the first given name and writes out the second given name in full. You should indicate in some way who is making the presentation. Typically this is done by underlining the presenter's name. The title slide should also indicate the affiliation of each coauthor. Typically this includes their department or research institute and their university, government laboratory, or company.

It is important that you number your slides, irrespective of whether it is a formal oral presentation or a poster. If you use PowerPoint to prepare your slides, choosing "insert slide number" will put the slide number in either the header or footer of the slide. The preferred location is in the lower right hand corner of the footer. You should begin numbering your slides with the title slide. This provides an opportunity for you to point out to the audience that the slides are numbered. Hence, if they have questions on a particular slide, they can refer to it by number. An option on the title slide is to use some simple animation to draw attention to the slide number. This could be a flashing circle encompassing the slide number that you activate by a "click." This animation of the slide number serves to remind you to point out to the audience that you have numbered your slides and also draws their attention to where you have numbered the slides.

3.3.2 What Else It Can Include

Optional components on the title slide are the forum and date of the presentation. The forum is the particular technical meeting, conference, symposium, etc., at which you are making the presentation. The date could either be the inclusive dates of the particular meeting, conference, symposium, etc., or the date on which you are making the presentation. Including the forum and date for your presentation can be helpful in the future when you want to find it on your computer or storage device for some purpose such as sending it to an interested person or using it to prepare another talk.

Another optional component on the title slide is your website address or that of your research group. This is an effective way to "advertise" for anyone, but in particular for young people who might be seeking a postdoctoral appointment, faculty position, or job in industry. You can also put your email address on the title slide. However, an alternative is to put your email address on the "Thank You" slide at the end of your talk. This will be discussed in Section 3.12, The "Thank You" Slide.

It is a good idea to include the logo of your university or company on your title slide. It is also a polite gesture to include the logo of the organization that is sponsoring the meeting at which you are presenting or hosting your presentation.

3.4 THE OUTLINE OR OVERVIEW

The outline or overview is usually a bulleted list of the major parts of your presentation. It would be included as a slide in a formal oral presentation but is optional for a poster although it can be helpful. The purpose of the outline or overview is to provide the audience with a "roadmap" of your talk.

The bullets are the milestones in your talk. Two important bullets are "Objectives" and "Conclusions." These bullets might consist of just the words "Objectives" or "Conclusions" without any information on what the objectives or conclusions are. When you go over your outline or overview, you should provide a few details on each of the bulleted components to show how your talk is organized.

3.5 THE INTRODUCTION

The introduction is an essential component in both formal oral and poster presentations. It usually requires more than one slide or poster panel. The introduction should give a brief background on the focus area of your presentation and should indicate why it is important. It should indicate the challenge or challenges that your presentation will address. Any special terminology such as acronyms and uncommon abbreviations should be defined. The introduction should lead to the objectives of the work that you are presenting. The objectives should follow naturally from an effective introduction and should be concise and descriptive. Avoid wordy objectives. Try to keep each objective to one line.

3.6 THE REVIEW OF PRIOR STUDIES

Including a review of prior studies in either a formal oral presentation or a poster is optional. You are the best judge as to whether this is necessary. A key consideration is whether omitting any reference to prior work will cause your audience to question your credibility.

There are two commonly used ways to handle a review of prior studies compactly. Either way usually can be done using only one or two slides or poster panels. One way is to have a slide that lists key papers and patents in chronological order (i.e., by date). Another way is to have a table that summarizes prior work. Remember that the purpose of prior studies is both to give credit to prior investigators for their work and to indicate the challenges that remain. Addressing these challenges provides the motivation for your study.

3.7 THE RESEARCH PLAN

3.7.1 Indicating the Design Considerations

Good practice is to begin by indicating the design considerations that had to be addressed in your research plan. For example, in an experimental study it might have been necessary to maintain isothermal conditions. Hence, your slide or poster panel that indicates the design considerations would have a bullet that states "*maintain isothermal conditions*". At this point in your presentation you do not indicate how in fact you maintained isothermal conditions. You merely state that this needed to be done. For a theoretical study a design consideration might have been to incorporate nonconstant physical properties. Hence, your slide or poster panel would have a bullet that states "*incorporate nonconstant physical properties*". When presenting this slide or discussing this poster panel, you would not indicate how you actually incorporated nonconstant physical properties.

3.7.2 Indicating How the Problem Will be Addressed

After indicating the design considerations, you need to provide an overview of the design and methodology for your study. This will usually require more than one slide or poster panel. The manner in which this material is presented differs depending on whether it is an experimental study or a theoretical development.

3.7.3 Research Plan for an Experimental Study

In some way you need to summarize the final design of the experimental study. This can be done using a schematic, photograph, or perhaps an animation of the apparatus. Many studies today involve micro- or nano-scale phenomena that preclude showing a meaningful actual photograph. In such cases an animation of the phenomena of interest might be an effective way to show your audience the methodology you used in your study. For example, assume that you used ultrasound (sound waves) to probe some phenomenon. Showing a photograph of an acoustic transducer (a piezoelectric crystal) or a trace of the ultrasound output (voltage versus time or frequency) might not be particularly illustrative or interesting for your audience. However, an animation showing how the sound waves created by an acoustic transducer propagate and are reflected as they pass through the media you studied can be very effective. Utilities such as PowerPoint permit you to animate schematics to create visuals that are far more effective than showing the actual apparatus.

For an experimental study it is important to summarize the design parameters and range of variables that were studied. The design parameters might be the constant temperature and pressure. In any experimental study one usually varies some parameters such as pressures, temperatures, concentrations, or flow rates over some range of values. This should be indicated on one slide or panel in your presentation. If it is not obvious how some parameter or variable was measured, this should be indicated in your presentation. For example, if one determined the average pore size in some porous medium such as a membrane, it is important to indicate how this was done, since the value might well depend on the characterization method that was used. In presenting an experimental study you might want to devote one slide or panel to summarizing the procedure you used in obtaining your data.

3.7.4 Research Plan for a Theoretical Development

Somewhat different considerations are involved in presenting a theoretical development. Including a slide or panel summarizing the design considerations is again recommended. You then need to summarize your approach to the theoretical development, preferably as a series of bullets. These bullets might include brief statements such as *"developed coupled mass and energy balances,"* or *"incorporated temperature-dependent physical properties,"* and a statement indicating how you solved the resulting system of equations. The latter could refer to the routine you developed to solve the problem or to a commercial code you used to solve a set of coupled differential equations or to do molecular dynamic simulations. It is important to include a slide or panel that summarizes the assumptions involved in your theoretical development. In a theoretical development it is usually necessary to include a few equations. Careful consideration should be given to keeping the number of equations to a minimum. Explaining complex equations within the span of the 15 or 20 minutes typically allowed for technical presentations is challenging even for experienced speakers. Remember that it is important to define all the symbols used in any equations in your slides or poster panels. In view of this, it is better to compress as much as possible of your theoretical development into brief narrative statements. For example, rather than giving the finite difference equations for some numerical solution to a problem, one might just say *"a central difference scheme was used."* A very effective way to present a complex solution methodology is to use a block diagram that illustrates the input, decision points, feedback loops, and output. Keep in mind when presenting a theoretical development that the audience will be most interested in your results rather than how you obtained them. If your results are interesting and significant, people will contact you or read your papers to obtain more information on the methodology that you used.

If you can't explain it simply, you don't understand it well enough.
—Albert Einstein, 1921 Nobel Laureate in Physics

3.8 THE DISCUSSION OF RESULTS

3.8.1 Showing Typical Results

It is important to realize that you will not be able to present all the results of your study within the time allowed for most presentations. Hence, you want to focus on typical results that are most significant. You need to plan your presentation to permit devoting several slides or poster panels to presenting your results, since this is the most important part of your talk. Your results can be presented as graphs, tables, photographs, micrographs, simulations, and digitized video clips.

3.8.2 Presenting Your Results

It is critical that you label all graphs, figures, micrographs, etc. clearly with large font. For example, micrographs obtained via scanning electron microscopy or atomic force microscopy usually have a micron or nanometer scale bar that is too small to be seen when inserted into one of your slides or poster panels. Hence, it is necessary to insert a scale bar that is easily readable for the audience. When presenting graphs, experimental as well as numerical simulation data should be shown via discrete points. In contrast, analytical solutions should be shown via continuous lines. When you put a line connecting your data points, you need to indicate how this line was determined. If the line is a best-fit determined via a least-squares minimization routine, you should indicate the coefficient-of-determination (COD). In presenting any photographs, micrographs, etc., you should always give some indication of the scale. This can be done by showing a familiar object such as a coin, paper clip, etc. that has a similar size in the same photo. However, the familiar object that you show for size comparison should not be distracting such that it draws attention away from what you want your audience to see.

3.8.3 Providing Some Measure of Reproducibility

It is important when presenting your data to indicate some measure of their replicability or reproducibility. This can be done by showing plots of replicate measurements, error bars, or via the results of statistical analysis of your data such as the standard error. It is important to indicate how many replicate measurements or remeasurements were done to determine the experimental error. You should also indicate whether you did remeasurements involving repeating the experiment with the same sample or whether you did replicate measurements involving repeating the experiment with different samples. Remeasurements include only the error integral to the apparatus and procedure, whereas replicate measurements include both the experimental error as well as any error introduced owing to variability in the samples.

We encounter regression to the mean almost every day of our lives. We should try to anticipate it, recognize it, and not be fooled by it.

Gary Smith, *Standard Deviations: Flawed Assumptions, Tortured Data, and Other Ways to Lie with Statistics*, ISBN13: 9781468309201, The Overlook Press, New York, 2014

3.8.4 Emphasizing Interesting Observations

In the limited time that you have to present your results, it is important that you devote one or more slides or poster panels to the interesting observations emanating from your data or model. You definitely should devote a slide or poster panel to the significance or novelty of your results.

3.9 THE CONCLUSIONS

Any technical presentation should have a concluding slide or poster panel. The conclusions preferably should be presented as bullets or as a numbered list. The conclusions should relate back to the objectives that you presented earlier in your presentation. There should be at least one conclusion for each of your stated objectives, even if the conclusion is that the stated objective could not be achieved. Since a well-posed study often leads to unanticipated discoveries, you sometimes will have more conclusions than stated objectives! Your conclusions should be concise. If possible, confine each conclusion to one line of text. If a conclusion goes beyond two lines, try to reword it to make it more compact. Your conclusions will be a large part of what your audience takes away from your presentation. Make them easily readable and understandable!

3.10 A FUTURE WORK SLIDE

It usually is not appropriate to include future work in presentations at technical meetings, conferences, and symposia. Including a slide or poster panel indicating future work is important in presentations such as thesis defenses, progress reviews, research-group seminars, job interview seminars, and reports on work being done under contract or for an employer. Future work can best be presented as one or two slides or poster panels consisting of succinct bullets or an itemized list indicating what will or can be done in the future.

3.11 THE ACKNOWLEDGMENTS

Any technical presentation should include an acknowledgments slide or panel. It is rare that any technical work could have been done without the help of other people, support facilities (e.g., an electron microscopy laboratory, instrument shop, etc.), or funding agencies. In particular, the acknowledgments should indicate any source of funding for the technical work such as grants or contracts as well as fellowships or scholarships awarded to any of the coauthors of the presentation. It is also appropriate and ethical to acknowledge any individuals who provided substantive assistance for the work you are presenting. These could be colleagues with whom you had helpful discussions of your work, people who provided samples that you used in your study, someone who edited or proofread your slides or poster panels, or people such as your research group who provided feedback when you practiced your presentation.

3.12 THE "THANK YOU" SLIDE

A "Thank You" slide or poster panel is a nice way to end your presentation, since it provides an opportunity for you to thank the audience for attending your presentation. This slide or poster panel might just say *"Thank You."* The "Thank You" slide or poster panel also provides an opportunity for you to end your presentation in a less formal way, perhaps by introducing some clip-art humor showing a comical character asking whether there are any questions! An example of this is given in the PowerPoint presentation that is available in the online materials for this guidebook. One reason for ending your presentation on a "lighter note" is to "soften up" your audience. This can be advantageous when you field questions by making the audience less critical. A speaker presenting a technical talk, particularly a formal oral presentation, usually projects a rather serious demeanor owing to the nature of the subject. By ending your talk less formally you convey a friendly and approachable personality that will be receptive to questions from the audience. Good advice is to include your email address on the "Thank You" slide or poster panel. If you have given a good presentation that has made a positive impression on the audience, some people might want to contact you regarding professional opportunities!

NOTES

26 Presenting an Effective and Dynamic Technical Paper

Chapter 4

Making a Formal Oral Presentation

The best way to make a good speech is to have a good beginning and a good ending — and have them close together.

—Author unknown

4.1 FOCUS AND SCOPE OF THIS CHAPTER

4.1.1 Importance of an Effective Presentation Style

An effective well-organized presentation engages the audience, motivates them by indicating the technical challenges that define the objectives, leads them through a logical overview of the research plan and procedure, excites them with a discussion of the results that underscores their significance, and impresses them with meaningful conclusions that relate back to the objectives. You might have put together a well-organized presentation and have very significant research results, but not be successful in engaging, motivating, exciting, and impressing the audience because of deficiencies in delivering your presentation. Whereas good organization is critical to having a logical flow in your presentation, a good talk must also embody the components of an effective delivery. This is the focus of this chapter.

4.1.2 Distinguishing Features of Making a Formal Oral Presentation

Delivering a formal oral presentation is quite different from giving a poster. The visuals for a formal oral presentation usually will be slides prepared via PowerPoint or similar utility for which you will be using an LCD (liquid-crystal display), DLP (digital light processor), or other projector. As such, your slides will be viewed sequentially. This provides for some options in the use of the background and color. For a formal oral presentation you will be the only one speaking to a captive audience and usually will speak without any interruptions. You might be confined to standing in front of a podium, and probably will be using a microphone and a laser pointer. Most importantly, there is a specified time for a formal oral presentation that includes the time allowed for questions. If you give your presentation within the allowable time, you will be able to entertain questions from the audience afterwards. However, the questions are handled in a formal manner with no time for any extended discussion. For these reasons this chapter will focus on delivering a formal oral presentation, whereas Chapter 5, Giving a Poster Presentation, will discuss giving a poster for which the format is considerably more informal.

4.1.3 Developing Your Own Presentation Style

It is important to emphasize that there are many ways to make a presentation. Indeed, you should strive to make your presentation style uniquely your own. Analogously to the manner in which each accomplished musician, painter, or poet makes their own unique artistic expression, so too your presentation style should evolve into an expression of your personality. Projecting your personality into your presentation skills should be done while observing the dictates of effective public speaking, which will be discussed in this chapter. However, since you have considerable latitude in developing your presentation style, this chapter also includes a variety of suggestions for accomplishing this. You should accept the suggestions that are most appealing to you and that you will be comfortable using in your presentation. Moreover, you are encouraged to develop your own techniques for enhancing your presentation skills. The Information Age is continually advancing new ways to make a technical presentation more engaging. In particular, new software is becoming available that can add a whole new dimension to the quality of your visuals!

4.2 PREPARING YOUR SLIDES

4.2.1 Preliminary Considerations in Preparing Your Slides

There is no question that PowerPoint has been at least a part of the problem because it has affected a generation. It should have come with a warning label and a good set of design instructions back in the '90s. But it is also a copout to blame PowerPoint — it's just software, not a method.
—Garr Reynolds, author of *Presentation Zen: Simple Ideas on Presentation Design and Delivery*, 2nd ed., ISBN13: 9780321811981, New Riders, Berkeley, CA, 2011

Once you know that your presentation has been accepted for a particular technical meeting, conference, symposium, etc., you need to prepare your slides. The terminology "slides" is a holdover from yesteryear. Prior to the development of digital imaging, presentations were made by projecting 35 mm color transparencies that were called "slides." Clearly you need to allow ample time for preparing your slides. If this will be the first formal presentation of the particular technical work, it will typically take several weeks to prepare your slides. This usually involves preparing slides via PowerPoint or some similar utility. The organization of your slides should follow the guidelines for organizing and outlining your presentation discussed in Chapter 3, Organizing Your Presentation. It is good practice to have a header for each of your slides such as "Overview," "Objectives," "Design Considerations," "Conclusions," etc. drawn from the major headings in your outline.

PowerPoint is the default in Microsoft Office and is the most widely used utility for preparing slide presentations. There are several alternative utilities for preparing your slides that include PowToon, Prezi, Keynote, Prezentit, Kingsoft Presentation Free, Haiku Deck, and others. These presentation utilities differ insofar as the platform for which they are designed (Windows, Mac, IPhone, Android, etc.), capabilities (e.g., 3-D animations), cost (some are free!), ease-of-use, and purpose (sales, marketing, technical presentations, etc.). In particular, utilities such as Cinema 4D Studio are finding increasing use for preparing attractive poster presentations. The development of presentation software is a very active area with new products continually entering the market. Check the web for information on the latest software and their ratings.

4.2.2 Making Your Visuals Easy to Understand

You should avoid complexity or too much material on any slide. Since the audience can read faster than you can speak, too much text on a single slide will inevitably cause them to read everything rather than listen to your discussion of the material. When it is necessary to have a lot of text on a slide, you can use animation in PowerPoint or similar utility to have successive lines "enter" upon a mouse click as they are discussed. If you do elect to use some animation feature such as "appear," "fade," "dissolve-in," etc. in PowerPoint, it is a good idea to have prior text on this slide disappear as the new material appears. This avoids cluttering up the slide with too much information. When using animation to introduce text, avoid the "exciting" entrance modes such as "bounce," "boomerang," "flip," etc. in PowerPoint, since they can be distracting to the audience. A similar consideration applies to having text disappear. The byword in preparing your presentation is to keep the slides as simple as possible to facilitate effective communication.

4.2.3 Choosing an Appropriate Font

It is recommended that you use one of the more simple fonts in preparing your visuals. Older versions of PowerPoint used "Times New Roman" as the default font. This is a more florid font that can be difficult to read particularly for people in the audience for whom English is not their first language. Simpler fonts such as "Arial," "Calibri (Body)," "Tahoma," "Verdana," and others are recommended. Newer versions of PowerPoint now use "Calibri (Body)" as the default font. In order to illustrate the difference between a florid and a simpler font, the same phrase will be written here using "Times New Roman" and "Calibri (Body)":

The visuals in your presentation should be easy to read.

versus.

The visuals in your presentation should be easy to read.

The differences between these two fonts are readily apparent. For example, the "T" in "Times New Roman" has "hooks" at the ends and bottom. The "T" in "Calibri (Body)" is simply two mutually perpendicular straight lines. Simplicity is the byword in choosing the font for your presentation.

4.2.4 Choosing an Appropriate Font Size

In preparing your slides for a formal oral presentation it is important to use a font size that can be read easily from the most distant point in the room where your audience will be seated. For this reason Section 2.3 underscored the importance of knowing something about the room for your presentation, in particular, its size. If you will be giving your talk in a large room, you will need to use an appropriately larger font size. If the room size is uncertain, it is always better to err on the side of using a larger font size. Using a larger font size of course presents the challenge of fitting all the required text onto the slide. Here again the use of animation to cause text to appear and disappear is very helpful.

4.2.5 Choosing an Appropriate Color Scheme

The lighting conditions in the room in which you will be making your presentation are important in choosing a color scheme for your slides. It usually is not possible to know the room lighting conditions prior to arriving on-site. If this is the case, you will need to choose a color scheme that will be effective irrespective of the lighting conditions. This somewhat limits your choice of background and font colors. For a formal oral presentation a color scheme for your slides that looks good in dim light might be totally washed out in brighter light. The emergence of high intensity LCD and DLP projectors has permitted the room lighting to be brighter. Hence, it is important to choose a color scheme appropriate to a reasonably well-lit room. It is good practice to preview the color scheme for your slides using an LCD or DLP projector in a reasonably well-lit room when you are preparing your presentation.

You want a good contrast between the colors you choose for your font and the background in your slides in order to make them easily readable. It is good practice to use dark fonts such as black or dark blue on softer, lighter backgrounds. Avoid sharply contrasting colors between the font and the background, since this can be very tiring on the eyes of the audience. It is also good practice to maintain a consistent color scheme for your slides in order to avoid giving the impression that you threw them together from different prior presentations in preparing your talk. Since your slides are presented one at a time in a formal oral presentation, you have the opportunity for an occasional departure from your color scheme for emphasis. For example, on the particular slide that summarizes the challenges that you addressed in your work, you might choose a color scheme in which the background is somewhat somber such as black. When presenting a slide showing some of your most significant results, you might want to use a brightly colored font such as red to subtly inject emphasis and to project excitement. You also can use color to harmonize with the subject of your talk. For example, if you are giving a presentation on research you did on seawater desalination, you might choose a light blue background suggestive of water. If your talk concerns some aspect of energy, you could use a suggestive background color such as yellow. If it involves some aspect of environment or ecology, you might use green. Use your imagination to use color for enhancing your presentation and more effectively communicating with your audience. Making your presentation visually attractive provides an opportunity for you to unleash your artistic talent along with the technical expertise that is embodied in your talk!

4.2.6 Emphasizing Important Parts of Your Presentation

Another way to emphasize the important parts of your presentation is to change the font color or font size. Both modes of emphasis can be done either statically or dynamically via animation. For example, you might list a series of design considerations for your experiment in a dark font and then indicate how you addressed these design considerations in a brighter font. A dynamic variation on the same slide might be to have the design consideration fade-out as the manner in which you addressed the design consideration fades-in perhaps in a different color font. An example of when you might use a larger font size is when you define acronyms such as SEM. An effective way to do this is to show the words "Scanning Electron Microscopy" in which you use larger font for the "S," "E," and "M" that define the acronym. Another example that uses a combination of animation and larger font size is when you have some equation that is pivotal to the technology that you are discussing. You might first introduce this equation using the same size font as the text on the particular slide. However, to emphasize the equation that underlies the technology that you are discussing, you can use the "zoom" utility in PowerPoint, activated by a mouse click, to enlarge the equation to occupy the full slide while fading out the other text on the slide.

4.2.7 Use of Animations and Sounds

Animations other than for introducing material sequentially in more detailed slides should be used sparingly, since they can distract the audience from paying attention to what you are trying to communicate to them. If you do use an animation, do not run it continuously. Have the animation repeat once or twice at most. One very good use of animations is to illustrate how an apparatus works. This can be far more effective than just showing a photograph or schematic of the apparatus. In general, sounds accompanying your slides should be avoided unless you have a very good reason for using them.

4.2.8 Choosing a Template

A template provides a format for your slides in terms of graphics, font size and color, and background color. PowerPoint and similar utilities have preloaded templates that you can choose for your slide presentation. You can edit the graphics, font, and color on a template by clicking the "Slide Master" tab in PowerPoint. You also can design your own template. Avoid templates that use up too much space on a slide. None of the text, figures, photos, graphs, etc. should spill over onto any part of the graphics on the template that you use. This makes the slide look sloppy. Avoid templates that are distracting in that they draw attention away from the content of your slides. An attractive template to use is one that promotes your organization. Many universities, research laboratories, and companies have templates readily available that you can download. Never use a template that in any way uses animation, since this will be a distraction to the audience.

4.2.9 Numbering Your Slides

It is important to number each slide in your presentation. This can be done by using the "insert page number" utility in PowerPoint (or similar utility) or by numbering the header for each slide. The "insert page number" utility has the advantage of automatically updating the slide number if you add or delete any slides. In contrast, if you choose to number the header of the slide, you need to renumber the slides if you add or delete any slides. Numbering your slides is both a courtesy and a convenience to the audience. In the event they have a question concerning one or more of your slides, it permits them to refer to them by number. When you have your title slide on the screen, it is important to tell the audience that you have numbered your slides so that they can refer to the slide by number if they have any questions. As mentioned in Section 3.3.1 on preparing your title slide, you might also use some animation such as a blinking circle around the number on the title slide to remind you to mention to the audience that your slides are numbered.

4.2.10 Proofreading Your Presentation

It is important to proofread your slides carefully. Do not trust "spell-check" or "grammar-check" utilities, since they check only whether there is a misspelled word or some grammatical error. They do not check whether the word is correct in the context of how you are using it. For example, you might have mistyped the word "from" as "form" or typed "the" instead of the intended word "then." A spell-check or grammar-check utility will not pick this up. If English is not your first language, you might want to have a native speaker proofread your slides.

You young people learned spelling by the 'Close Enough' method.
—Garrison Keillor, American humorist

4.3 SCOPING OUT THE ROOM AND FACILITIES WHEN ON-SITE

4.3.1 Scoping Out the Room for Your Presentation

One of the things mentioned in Chapter 2, Preliminary Considerations, concerning what needs to be done prior to preparing your presentation is to determine the venue. Often the information you can obtain prior to arriving on-site for your talk is quite limited. Hence, it is a good idea to arrive on-site well before the time of your presentation. If at all possible, visit the room in which you will be making your presentation to assess its geometry, lighting conditions, and other facilities. Knowing the layout of the room beforehand is particularly important in determining what you might need to do for effective eye contact during your presentation. More will be said about this in Section 4.5.3.

4.3.2 Scoping Out the Facilities for Your Presentation

Determine if you will have a microphone. If so, find out whether it will be fixed on a podium or will be the clip-on type that can be attached somewhere on your attire. If the microphone is fixed on a podium, you will be constrained to stand at the podium. This limits incorporating certain style elements into your talk. If the microphone is the clip-on type, you need to think about where you will carry the transmitter. Ways to cope with this were discussed in Section 2.6. More will be said about using a microphone in Section 4.4.1.

It is important to determine if a laser pointer will be provided. If not, you will need to bring your own. In fact, it is a good idea to bring your own laser pointer even if one will be provided. Section 4.4.2 will also say more about using a laser pointer.

You also need to determine whether you or a projectionist will control advancing the slides. You also might have to control the room illumination. If so, learn how to control the lighting. In particular, you might want to dim the room lights for low contrast slides such as electron, atomic force, laser confocal, or other imaging micrographs. Knowing how to control the microphone volume can also be useful, since it might have to be adjusted depending on how loudly you speak.

The organizers for technical meetings and conferences usually require that you load your slides onto the computer that is provided prior to the beginning of the session. In the case of invited seminars, job interviews, and other presentations of this type, you might need to bring your laptop computer. It is good practice to have your presentation not only loaded onto your laptop computer, but also to have it on a thumb drive in the event that there are problems with the computer that require switching to another one.

If at all possible, you should preview your presentation on the computer you will be using for your presentation. This is important to do if you will be making your presentation on a different computer than the one you used when preparing your slides. A utility such as MathType that is used for formatting equations might not project them correctly if it is not loaded onto the computer that you use for your presentation. Many technical meeting sites will have a special room for previewing your presentation. Sometimes it is possible to preview your slides in the room in which your talk will be given. If you do this, avoid having anyone else see your slides while you are previewing them. You do not want to disclose any part of your presentation to anyone in the audience prior to giving it. This can be done by toggling the appropriate function key on the computer to enable viewing your slides only on the computer screen rather than projecting it onto the screen in the room.

4.4 USE OF A MICROPHONE AND LASER POINTER

4.4.1 Use of a Microphone

Make certain that you stand at a proper distance from a fixed microphone on a podium. If the microphone is attached on your attire, locate it 20−25 cm (8−10 in.) below your mouth. If the microphone is fixed on a podium, you must stand in front of it throughout your talk. In contrast, a clip-on microphone allows you to move around, which permits you to use more body language to enhance your presentation. Usually the microphone on a podium is adjustable. Make certain that you adjust it for your height. Before you begin your presentation, ask the audience if they can hear you well. When doing so, make certain that people at the back of the room confirm that they can hear you well. Of course thank them for their response!

Since a microphone fixed to a podium is very directional, your voice will be louder when speaking directly into it than when you speak with your head turned to one side. This can cause variations in the volume of your voice that can be annoying to the audience. There is a range of about 25−40 cm (10−16 in.) from a microphone fixed on a podium within which the amplification of your voice will be optimal. Standing too far away from the microphone will reduce the volume of your voice. However, standing too close to the microphone can cause undesired distortion of consonants. For example, if you are too close to the microphone, pronouncing words beginning with the letters "b" and "p" can cause an exaggerated boom-type sound.

If you need to cough or sneeze while using a microphone, turn away from it in order to avoid amplifying a very distracting noise. Of course if you do have to cough or sneeze, it is polite to say "excuse me" to the audience.

Sometimes you will have the option of using either a clip-on microphone or a microphone fixed on a podium. Using a clip-on microphone gives you more options in terms of injecting body language into your presentation. If you use a clip-on microphone, either turn off the microphone on the podium or stand sufficiently far from it to avoid any "cross-talk" between the two microphones.

4.4.2 Use of a Laser Pointer

Most laser pointers today are also laser remotes that can control advancing the slides. If a laser pointer or laser remote is provided for your technical session, learn how to use it before giving your presentation. Prematurely pressing the button that advances the slides or worse yet, pressing the wrong button, can be distracting for the audience and break the flow of your presentation. It also can contribute to making you nervous. If possible, use your own laser pointer, since you will be familiar with its operation and less likely to press the wrong button. Moreover, the laser pointer provided for your session might malfunction owing to weak batteries.

If you do not have your own laser pointer, consider purchasing one that also will advance the slides. Avoid purchasing a laser remote with too many features, since it presents more opportunities for pressing the wrong button. The essential features for a laser remote are the ability to advance and reverse the slides, and to blank the screen. The newer and more expensive green laser pointers are an order-of-magnitude brighter than the older red laser pointers. These are particularly effective when the screen and room lighting are very bright. Laser remotes are now available that include a memory chip that allows you to store your presentation on the device. This is a nice feature that does not affect its use during your presentation. When purchasing your own laser remote, you should consider its ergonomic design. Choose one that you can hold easily in the palm of your hand so that you can use both hands for appropriate positive body language to enhance your presentation.

Note that many laser remotes require inserting the transmitter into a UCB port on the computer, although some do not require this. Remember to remove the transmitter after your presentation! It is also a good idea to carry extra batteries for your laser pointer or laser remote, since the batteries only die when you are using them! Note that the brighter green laser pointers use battery power much faster than the less bright red laser pointers.

4.5 MASTERING THE MECHANICS OF AN EFFECTIVE ORAL PRESENTATION

4.5.1 Your Appearance

You never get a second chance to make a first impression.
—Paul Kirk, former US Democratic National Committee Chairman

Section 2.6 discusses a critical element in making a positive impression. The impression that you make also relates to avoiding distracting mannerisms such as slouching, shuffling your feet, and awkward gestures such as scratching your head, running your fingers through your hair, adjusting your glasses, playing with the laser pointer, etc. It is also important that you do not eat or chew on anything during your presentation. In particular, chewing gum creates a very bad impression!

4.5.2 Vocalization

These are the three things — volume of sound, modulation of pitch, and rhythm that a speaker bears in mind. It is those who do bear them in mind who usually win prizes in the dramatic contests.
—Aristotle, Greek philosopher, 384−322 BC

Speaking sufficiently loud is easier for men, who usually have deeper and louder voices, than for women. For this reason women need to work on projecting their voice. Needless to say, if people cannot hear you well, you will not communicate to them. Use a microphone if it is available. This applies to both men and women. Often men think that their voice is sufficiently loud so that they do not need a microphone. They start off their presentation appropriately speaking with a louder voice than they would use in normal conversation. However, as they get into their talk, they sometimes forget to continually elevate the volume of their voice and revert back to a speaking volume more appropriate for conversation than for a formal oral presentation in a large room. Hence, use a microphone if it is available.

As mentioned in Section 4.4.1 it is good practice before you begin your presentation to direct a question to the audience asking whether they can hear you well. In particular, this question should be directed to people sitting at the back of the room. When people respond to this question, you should thank them.

Avoid speaking in a monotone voice by using voice inflections occasionally. Monotone speaking in Western cultures can convey a lack of enthusiasm in the speaker. This is not what you want to project to your audience. Speakers from Western cultures tend to use more voice inflection in their presentations than speakers from many non-Western cultures. However, today we face the challenge of speaking to global audiences. Using voice inflection will not in any way detract from your presentation to a multicultural audience that includes people from non-Western cultures. In contrast, speaking in a monotone voice could create a negative impression on people in the audience from Western cultures. Hence, use voice inflections to emphasize certain points in your talk such as significant results. Voice inflections do not necessarily imply increasing the volume of your voice. Sometimes lowering the volume of your voice can be used to get people to pay very close attention to what you are saying.

The right word may be effective, but no word was ever as effective as a rightly timed pause.

—Mark Twain, American humorist

Another useful speaking technique is to use the pause occasionally. This is particularly effective after you direct a rhetorical question to the audience. This is a question you ask the audience that you do not expect them to answer. More will be said about rhetorical questions in Section 4.6.2. By pausing after a rhetorical question, you give the audience a few seconds to think about the question before you answer it for them.

This guidebook has a particular focus for speakers whose first language is not English. Many readers might speak English with a bit of an accent. This should not cause any undue concern. Native speakers from the United Kingdom, Australia, New Zealand, South Africa, and the United States speak English with markedly different accents! Many of us whose first language is English enjoy listening to a non-native speaker give a presentation in English. A bit of an accent when speaking English makes it more pleasing to the ear of most native speakers and also adds a bit of sophistication! If English is not your first language, you should speak more slowly during your presentation, since some people in the audience will have to adjust to your accent. Note that this applies as well to native English speakers from different English-speaking countries. For example, many people from the United States have difficulty understanding speakers from Australia, New Zealand, and the United Kingdom. Undoubtedly the converse is true as well! Speaking more slowly takes some practice, particularly in maintaining a slower speaking pace throughout your talk.

4.5.3 Effective Eye Contact

So much is said with the electricity of the eyes, the intensity of a whisper. Less is more.

—Elizabeth Taylor, Academy-Award-winning actress

Whether you are giving a formal oral presentation or a poster, you need to be aware of effective eye contact with your audience. However, this is handled differently in Western cultures than in some Asian cultures. In Western cultures eye contact conveys sincerity and an indication of your interest in communicating directly with each person in the audience. However, in some Asian cultures direct eye contact, in particular with someone who is senior to you in either age or position, can be an affront. Indeed, in some Asian cultures when meeting someone senior in age or position, deference is shown by casting one's eyes slightly downward. The challenge then is how to handle eye contact when you are addressing a multicultural audience. If you are addressing a small multicultural audience, you should have direct eye contact with people you know are from a Western culture.

However, look toward but not directly at people from Asian countries for which direct eye contact is not culturally acceptable. The problem is sometimes you really do not know whether someone in the audience is from a country for which direct eye contact is an issue. If you are from a Western culture and have direct eye contact with someone from an Asian country for whom direct eye contact would normally be avoided, they probably will not be offended. However, if you are from an Asian country for which direct eye contact is an issue, avoid having it with anyone in the audience from the same culture who is senior in age or position. You are expected to understand the customs of your culture. When in doubt regarding using direct eye contact with individuals in a small audience, take in the entire audience by looking around the room while avoiding any direct eye contact with anyone you think might be offended. Things are much easier when you are addressing a large multicultural audience. A useful technique is to identify five people located at the four corners and middle of the room. It helps if you know these people, since you are less likely to forget their faces. You then need to remind yourself to look toward each of these five people periodically throughout your talk. In doing so, you will be engaging your entire audience with effective eye contact while not having direct eye contact with any particular individual.

When giving a formal oral presentation, standing to the right of the screen while you face the audience has the tendency to minimize eye contact with the audience to your right. Standing to the left of the screen while you face the audience minimizes eye contact with the audience to your left. Hence, if you stand to the right of the screen while facing the audience, be aware to maintain good eye contact with the audience on your right. Conversely if you stand to the left of the screen while facing the audience, be aware to maintain good eye contact with the audience on your left.

Be careful that you do not continuously look at your slides on the screen. Look to see what is on the screen and then turn to your audience to discuss it. This is much easier to do if you are thoroughly familiar with the flow of your presentation so that you can anticipate your next slide. Mastering the flow of your presentation is facilitated by preparing a good outline for your talk as was discussed in Section 2.5. Maintaining a good balance between looking at the screen and maintaining eye contact with your audience is made easier by positioning your body at an angle of 30–45 degrees relative to the plane of the screen so that you are always partially facing the audience. Alternatively when you have a clip-on microphone, you can move about a bit to look at the screen occasionally and to engage your audience via effective eye contact. Moving about during your presentation takes a bit more courage, but can be very effective. Practice this when giving less formal presentations such as for your research group. With a bit of practice you can become quite comfortable doing it!

4.5.4 Body Language

Body language in the context of a presentation relates to how consciously or subconsciously you use your hands, posture, and body movement. You want your body language to be a positive complement to your oral presentation. Hence, you should assume a professional posture. Avoid slouching, shuffling, putting your hands in your pockets, and other undesirable negative body motions. Do not engage in awkward mannerisms such as scratching your head, adjusting your glasses, playing with the laser pointer, etc. Avoid body language that sends the wrong message such as a clenched fist. If possible, have someone digitally record you while making a formal oral presentation so that you can see your body language. Viewing your digital recording can be an eye-opening experience, since many of us have mannerisms during our speaking of which we are totally unaware. Not all mannerisms are necessarily bad. However, some can be distracting to your audience. More will be said about digitally recording your talk prior to your presentation in Section 4.8.

You should not be afraid to use your hands during either a formal oral presentation or a poster. Your hands can be used to show size, direction, and motions related to how something happens. They also can be used to convey emotions. For example, outstretched hands with your palms facing upward connote offering something for acceptance by the audience. Outstretched hands with both palms turned inwards can convey the notion that something can be done or that something is possible. Since your hands can be a very effective part of your body language, you do not want to encumber them. Usually you will have a laser remote in one hand. You do not want to encumber your other hand by having to hold the transmitter for the clip-on microphone. Hence, as mentioned in the Section 2.6 you need to make certain that you have some type of pocket for the microphone transmitter.

Your body language can include moving around a bit during a formal oral presentation. In particular, moving from one side of the screen to the other is an effective way to ensure that you are engaging the audience on both sides of the room. Moving toward the audience in a small room can be effective in engaging them. However, moving around can be done only if you have a clip-on microphone or if you are in a small room and do not require a microphone.

4.5.5 Use of Humor

> *The human race has one really effective weapon, and that is laughter.*
> —Mark Twain, American humorist

Introducing humor in some form in a formal oral presentation is somewhat of a cultural thing. Speakers from Western cultures tend to use it far more than those from Eastern Europe, the Middle East, Asia, or Africa. Surprisingly people from all cultures seem to enjoy humor when it is done in good taste and in moderation. In general, one should avoid humor involving politics, gender, race, religion, or sexual orientation. Avoid any humor that has any element of vulgarity, since it undoubtedly will offend some people in the audience.

Humor can be introduced into a presentation either verbally or via one's slides. Clip-art is an effective way to introduce humor into a talk without the need to say anything about it. A good way to introduce humor verbally is to use a quotation from a famous person, a familiar adage, a poem, or a quip. For example, when you have a momentary lapse-of-memory, a quip such as *"Funny, I don't remember being absent-minded."* Or when you make a mistake in something you say, a good quip is: *"What I said is a good example of the 50-50-90 rule: Anytime you have a 50-50 chance of getting something right, there's a 90% probability you'll get it wrong!"* If something really goes wrong during your presentation such as a failure of the LCD or DLP projector, you might say something like the following taken from Mark Twain, the master of one-liner quips: *"Perhaps I should have followed Mark Twain's advice who said If you eat a frog first thing in the morning the rest of the day will be much better!"*

It is usually difficult to find just the right quotation, adage, poem, clip-art, etc. when you need it. Hence, it is a good idea when you find good material for your presentations to store it in an electronic file on your computer.

4.5.6 Handling a Momentary Lapse-of-Memory

When I was younger I could remember anything, whether it happened or not; but I am getting old, and soon I shall remember only the latter.

—Mark Twain, American humorist

Even experienced speakers sometimes are confronted with a momentary lapse-of-memory such that they cannot remember what they wanted to say. The author has found that these momentary memory lapses occur more frequently with advancing age! These unpleasant moments can be minimized by having a well-organized talk. In particular, if you have prepared an outline for your presentation, you know the flow of the material that you want to present. However, in spite of preparing well for your talk, the excitement of being before an audience might cause you to forget where you are in your talk. This is where having the cue cards discussed in Section 2.5 will be very helpful. If you do momentarily forget what comes next or what you wanted to say at some point in your talk, avoid using awkward interjections such as "ah" or "um." These grunts and groans will indicate to the audience that you are having a problem. If your cue cards are sufficiently small, you can slip them out of your pocket for quick reference without causing any noticeable distraction for the audience. When you practice your talk and find that you do have a problem at one or more points such as not being able to remember some highly technical word, make a note on your cue cards to help you if this same problem occurs during your presentation. If you are well-prepared for your talk, you probably will not need to take out your cue cards. However, it is worth repeating that knowing you have these cue cards in your pocket will bolster your confidence in delivering your presentation seamlessly even if you do have a momentary lapse-of-memory!

Having a momentary lapse-of-memory also can provide an opportunity to introduce a bit of humor into your presentation by injecting some short quip that you have practiced for such an occasion. For example, when I cannot remember what I wanted to say at some point in a talk that I am giving, I sometimes say *"At my age I am allowed to have a "senior moment" and I am using this opportunity to have one now!"* This will get the audience to laugh and turn an awkward moment into a positive one. Indeed, everyone enjoys a good laugh! A possible quip for younger speakers who encounter a memory lapse might be *"My grandfather used to tell me about having a senior moment when he could not remember something—I am practicing for my old age right now!"* This will cause the audience to laugh and allow you to relax a bit. It also gives you a few seconds to look at your cue cards and gather your thoughts to continue your presentation. Using cue cards and injecting some humor when you have a memory lapse during your presentation will impress the audience with how professionally you handled the situation.

4.6 STEPPING THROUGH YOUR PRESENTATION

I do not object to people looking at their watches when I am speaking. But I do strongly object when they start shaking them to make sure they are still going.

—Lord Birkett, 20th century British barrister noted for his skill as a speaker

4.6.1 Your Introduction by the Session Chair or Host

When giving a formal oral presentation you will be introduced by the session chair, cochair, or your host. They will introduce you by name and usually will give the title of your talk. They might also indicate the names of any coauthors for your presentation. If your name is difficult to pronounce, the person who introduces you might mispronounce it and thereby cause some laughter in the audience. You do not want to start your talk with any unintended laughter. Hence, to avoid this problem, it is a good idea before your introduction to indicate to the person who will introduce you how to pronounce your name. This could be done by giving them a small card with your name spelled out phonetically (i.e., as it sounds rather than the way it is spelled).

After being introduced you should thank by name (pronounced correctly!) whoever introduced you. In view of this, you should learn how to pronounce the name of the person who will introduce you. If you mispronounce their name and evoke laughter from the audience, it could be an unnerving way to begin your presentation.

Do not repeat your name or the title of your presentation if the person who introduced you did this. You might also briefly acknowledge the organizers of the particular conference, symposium, etc., or the person(s) who invited you to speak at this event. If the person who introduced you did not mention the coauthors on your presentation, it is proper to acknowledge them.

If you will be using a clip-on microphone, you should help the person who introduces you to clip it onto your apparel. Women should clip on the microphone if the person who introduces them is a man. This will avoid a possible embarrassing situation that again could evoke unintended laughter from the audience.

As mentioned in Section 4.5.2, before beginning your talk ask the audience if they can hear you well. You also should indicate to the audience that your slides are numbered so that if they have a question on a particular slide, they can refer to it by number. As suggested in Section 4.2.9, it is a good idea to use some simple animation such as a blinking circle around the page number on the title slide in order to draw attention to it.

4.6.2 Generating Interest Early in Your Presentation

It is important to engage the interest of the audience at the beginning of your presentation. Consider beginning with something provocative that will excite the audience in a positive way. For example, you might begin a talk on developing a hydrogen-energy economy with a provocative statement such as "*Do you know that if we do not develop a safe and economic method for hydrogen production within the next 10 years, none of us will be driving a car in 25 years!"* A talk on global climate change might begin with a graph showing the increase in carbon dioxide in the atmosphere that shows it is now at the highest in the past 700,000 years (based on the Greenland ice cores)! A talk involving technology to help developing countries might begin with a graph showing the exponential growth in world population. A talk on some aspect of water might begin with a provocative statement such as *"Did you know that one in seven people in the world does not have access to potable water?"*

I love fools' experiments. I am always making them.
—Charles Darwin, British naturalist and evolutionist

Another way to begin your presentation is with a rhetorical question. This is a question that you ask the audience but answer yourself. For example, a talk involving the development of a new portable oxygenator for people suffering from Chronic Obstructive Pulmonary Disease (COPD) might begin with the rhetorical question *"How would you solve the problem of COPD patients needing oxygen traveling on commercial airlines?"* A talk on global warming might begin with the rhetorical question *"How would you minimize greenhouse gas emissions without severely jeopardizing the world economy?"* A talk on some medical technology for birth control might begin with the rhetorical question *"How would you propose addressing exponential population growth with due consideration for different religious beliefs?"*

You also can begin with a bit of humor that will help you to relax. For example, when beginning a presentation on research that led to a significant advance you might begin with a statement such as "*Sir Isaac Newton* said *No great discovery was ever made without a bold guess—the research that I want to discuss with you also involved a few bold guesses—I will let you judge its significance!"*

Another way to begin your presentation is with a provocative image. For example, for a talk on drug-delivery show the size of a MEMS (MicroElectroMechanical Systems) device for delivering pharmaceuticals next to a familiar object such as a coin. For a talk on global warming show a dramatic photograph of the calving (breaking off of chucks) of glaciers in the high Arctic.

Begin your talk dynamically and as flawlessly as possible. However, you usually will be most nervous when you begin your presentation. Hence, it is a good idea to memorize the exact words you will use to begin your presentation (quote, humorous adage, some description of an image, etc.). You should write these words on your cue cards in case you have a memory lapse at the beginning of your presentation.

Clearly whatever quote, quip, or provocative image you use must tie in with the subject of your presentation. It is difficult to find the right material when you need it. A helpful recommendation is to create an electronic file on your computer of provocative quotations, humorous adages, meaningful graphs, and photographs that you can use as a resource when you need material of this type.

4.6.3 Pacing Your Presentation

Pacing your presentation means being aware of where you are in delivering the material that you want to present. It is critical that you either wear a watch or be able to see a clock in the room in which you are speaking so that you are aware of the time. Moreover, you need to know how much time you want to allocate to each part of your talk. A good "rule-of-thumb" is to allocate an average of 1 minute for each slide. This rule is based on counting all your slides including the title slide, acknowledgments, and "Thank You" slide on which you might spend only a few seconds. In general, you should reach the point where you state your objectives one-quarter to one-third of the way into your talk. Remember that the principal part of a technical talk should be your results and conclusions. Hence, be certain to allow ample time to discuss them. Look at the time throughout your presentation to make certain that you are "on schedule." Looking at a clock that is clearly visible in the room is better than having to look at your watch periodically. Never run over your time limit even if keeping on schedule requires that you delete material from your presentation.

To make a speech immortal, you don't have to make it everlasting.
—Author unknown

Some professional organizations use a warning-light system for formal oral presentations. This system is usually located on the podium so that you can easily see it. The session chair or cochair will tell you about the warning light system before your talk. They will indicate that you will receive a warning when you have only a few minutes remaining to finish your presentation. Typically a green light is lit when you begin your talk. A yellow light will appear a few minutes before your talk should end. This can range between 1 and 5 minutes. When the red light appears, the session chair or cochair will indicate that your time is up and will stop you irrespective of where you are in your presentation. It creates a very poor impression if you exceed your allotted time and cannot finish discussing the results or summarizing the conclusions.

4.6.4 Ending Your Presentation

No one ever complains about a speech being too short!
—Ira Hayes, Native American, one of the six marines who raised the US flag on Iwo Jima in WW II

It is a good idea to have a "Thank You" slide. This is a nice way to end your talk on a "lighter note" with some humor. For example, your "Thank You" slide might show a cartoon or clip-art picture of a speaker profusely perspiring and wiping their brow in relief after finishing. The slide should also have the words "Thank You" perhaps coming from the mouth of the cartoon character. A "Thank You" slide of this type is shown at the end of the PowerPoint presentation available with the online materials for this guidebook.

If you have not thanked the organizers of the meeting, conference, symposium, etc. or your host for the opportunity to make your presentation, you should do so when showing the "Thank You" slide. You should thank the audience for their attendance and attention. You should invite questions if they are allowed. Be aware that for formal oral presentations, recognizing questions from the audience is usually handled by the session chair or cochair.

It is important to put your contact information, in particular an email address, at the bottom of the "Thank You" slide. You might also include the URL (Uniform Resource Locator) for your web site or that of your research group. If you have given a good talk, someone in the audience might be interested in learning more about your background and contacting you about job opportunities. It pays to advertise!

4.6.5 Handling Questions Including Those You Cannot Answer

Find out in advance of giving your talk whether questions from the audience will be handled by you or the person running the session or your host. If the room is large and the people asking questions do not have access to a microphone, always repeat the question. This is a courtesy to the audience. Thank the person asking the question. Perhaps add a compliment such as *"That is a very good observation."* Repeating the question, thanking the questioner, and complimenting the questioner also gives you a few more seconds to generate an answer to the question! Be brief in answering questions to permit fielding as many as possible. Avoid arguments or protracted discussion with people asking questions. If disagreement arises, suggest that you can discuss the issue with the questioner after the session or via email.

Do not be embarrassed to say that you do not know the answer to a question. If one of your coauthors (e.g., your research advisor) is in the audience who might be able to answer the question, refer it to them. This means that you need to know where they are sitting in the audience! It is a good idea to have some arrangement with your coauthors or research advisor in the audience whereby they can give you a signal that they can help with answering the question. Do not refer a question to your advisor or coauthors in the audience without some sign from them that they want to entertain the question. If you defer a question to them that they cannot answer, it will be embarrassing for them.

If you cannot answer a question and no one is in the audience who can help you, ask the questioner to give you their business card after the session so that you can get back to them with an answer. Of course you need to follow up on this by contacting them as soon as possible after you have obtained the answer to their question.

4.7 HANDLING NERVOUSNESS

The human brain starts working the moment you are born and never stops until you stand up to speak in public.
—George (Georgie) Jessel, Academy-Award-winning movie producer

4.7.1 Channeling Nervousness Into Projecting Excitement

The question that I am asked most often during my oral communication skills workshops is how to handle nervousness. This is the uneasy state-of-mind that can occur when making a presentation. You need to realize that everyone, including experienced speakers, becomes a bit nervous when giving a talk. Nervousness is a manifestation of the excitement that you experience when making a presentation. If handled properly, it can be channeled into excitement that you project to your audience in a very positive way! Do not be concerned if English is not your first language and you speak with an accent. Believe it or not, as was mentioned in Section 4.5.2 most people whose first language is English enjoy hearing English spoken with an accent! Hence, there is no reason that speaking with an accent should cause you any nervousness. Use your accent as an asset in your speaking. Being multilingual is an accomplishment for which you should be proud!

There are only two types of speakers in the world: the nervous and the liars.
—Mark Twain, American humorist

A concern is projecting your nervousness to the audience that can make them uncomfortable. They will empathize with you because you are experiencing some anxiety. Nervousness should be projected positively into excitement rather than negatively into uneasiness for the audience. Try to reduce any manifestations of nervousness as much as possible. We will consider various techniques here that can be used to do this.

4.7.2 Ways to Control Nervousness

I like to smile. I smile even when I'm nervous since it calms me down and shows my friendliness.
—Yani Tseng, Youngest professional golfer ever to win five major championships

You need to believe that nervousness can be channeled into being a positive statement of the excitement you have in giving a talk. The first step in controlling nervousness is to remind yourself that for most technical presentations you are an authority in the field that you are talking about. Hence, you have no reason to be afraid. It might seem silly to suggest that you need to watch what you eat before giving a presentation. Some foods are not easily digested when you are excited and can cause you added discomfort. Having a glass of water on the podium or table near you can help control the "dry mouth" that sometimes accompanies nervousness. One visible sign of nervousness is causing the laser pointer to wiggle owing to your shaking hand. Avoid this by holding the laser pointer with two hands. Sometimes introducing humor early in your talk to connect with your audience helps to relax you as well. Introducing humor into your talk was discussed in Section 4.5.5. A way to gain confidence for your presentation is to ask one or more questions of the prior speakers in your session after their presentations. Hearing yourself ask a question when in the audience can make it easier when you have to speak before the audience. Another way to relax is to smile occasionally at people in the audience whom you know. These people will inevitably smile back to you, which will be reassuring for you. Smiling is like a rubber ball—it will bounce back to you! A very effective way to combat nervousness is to begin your talk in a provocative way that will energize the audience and grab their attention. A provocative introduction or "show stopper" at the beginning of your talk will immediately engage the audience in a way that you will recognize. This will bolster your confidence in moving into the body of your presentation.

4.7.3 Handling Mistakes That Cause Nervousness

To make no mistakes is not in the power of man; but from their errors and mistakes the wise and good learn wisdom for the future.
—Plutarch, Greek biographer 45–120 AD

Avoiding all mistakes in a presentation is virtually impossible. I do not recall ever giving a presentation in which I did not make several mistakes. Hence, you need to be ready to handle mistakes in a professional manner that will not make your audience feel uncomfortable. If you make an awkward mistake, you can use the occasion to introduce spontaneous humor as was discussed in Section 4.5.5. This is easier to do for speakers from Western cultures than for speakers from some non-Western cultures. For example, if I state something incorrectly in a talk, I sometimes inject the comment *"Oh, I forgot to tell you that you should not pay attention to what I am saying but should focus on what I am thinking—what I was thinking was ….."* I then correct the error that I made. This gets the audience to laugh since they certainly cannot focus on what I was thinking and puts both them and me at ease. As mentioned in Section 4.5.5, it is a good idea to develop some "one-liners" that you can "pull up" when you need them for these unanticipated awkward moments such as stating something incorrectly or having a momentary memory lapse.

4.7.4 The Easiest Way to Avoid Nervousness

The easiest way to avoid nervousness is to practice public speaking as often as you can. Look for opportunities to present your work. Begin with less formal events such as research group meetings and regional conferences and work up to international meetings and symposia. When possible, make poster rather than formal oral presentations at your first few major meetings or conferences. As you gain more experience in public speaking, you will not only be looking for opportunities to present your work, but will be sought after as an invited speaker at technical meetings and conferences.

A final bit of advice regarding controlling nervousness is to keep in mind that giving a presentation is your chance to "shine." Take full advantage of every opportunity that you have to make a presentation and enjoy every minute of it! Giving a formal oral presentation can really be a very enjoyable experience!

4.8 PRACTICE MAKES PERFECT

Practice does not make perfect since nobody is perfect. Practice does make better!
—Author unknown

It is important that you practice your talk several times prior to when it is scheduled to be given. One way to do this is to digitally record yourself giving the presentation. This is easy to do now using laptops, tablets, and smart phones that have built-in high-definition cameras. If possible, you should digitally record your presentation before an audience such as your research group, company team, or group of friends. It can be difficult when viewing a digital recording of your presentation to determine the effectiveness of your eye contact, body language, and integration of what you say with the slides that you are presenting. Hence, having an audience for your digital recording provides an opportunity for you to obtain feedback on these elements of an effective presentation. When you practice your talk, you might consider giving the people in the audience copies of the "Considerations when Critiquing a Presentation" that is available in Appendix D. In order to build your confidence immediately before or on the day of your presentation, you can practice your talk a few more times by giving it before a mirror in your room.

4.9 CRITIQUING PRESENTATIONS MADE BY OTHERS

An effective way to improve your presentation skills is to critique talks made by others. You know when someone has given a very good presentation. However, often it is not obvious why a presentation was not effective. Hence, you need to learn how to "reverse-engineer" a talk given by someone else. That is, you need to know how to break down a talk into its elements to determine how effective they were. An analogy here is listening to music. You know when you enjoy particular music. Most of us listen to music without thinking of why we enjoy it. However, aspiring musicians will analyze a great piece of music to develop an understanding of what makes it so wonderful. This same approach can be used to improve your presentation skills. In critiquing someone's presentation you need to be aware of the various elements of organization and style that are integral to an effective talk. It is good practice to critique not only excellent talks, but also to analyze why some presentations are less effective. Appendix D includes a critique sheet that I developed for the workshop that I teach on oral communication skills. Each student in the workshop is required to give a 15-minute digitally recorded presentation that is critiqued anonymously by the other students using this critique sheet. These critique sheets then are given to the student presenter to provide constructive feedback.

4.10 DEVELOPING YOUR PRESENTATION STYLE

Developing your presentation style is an evolutionary process. If your natural personality is to be a bit withdrawn, start modestly to develop a more outgoing and persuasive presentation style by introducing just a few of the suggestions in this chapter. As you become more comfortable with presentation skills, you can progressively add more. When you attend a dynamic and effective seminar or presented paper, you can "reverse-engineer" the presentation to pick out style elements that made the talk so impressive for you. The web provides another rich source of material to help you improve your presentation skills. Appendix E gives the URL for talks by four particularly effective speakers. You can view and "reverse-engineer" these and other presentations on the web to determine why they are so effective. If you are committed to becoming a "world-class" speaker, you will spend the rest of your professional life developing your presentation style!

NOTES

Chapter 5

Giving a Poster Presentation

5.1 FOCUS AND SCOPE OF THIS CHAPTER

5.1.1 Distinguishing Features of a Poster Presentation

Preparing and presenting a poster is markedly different than for a formal oral presentation. Hence, we begin with a discussion of the distinguishing features of a poster presentation. We need to introduce some definitions to distinguish between the panels for a poster and the slides for a formal oral presentation. Each slide in a formal oral presentation is projected sequentially onto a screen by an LCD or DLP projector. In contrast, a poster presentation will involve a "poster board" that will be set up for you by the session organizers in the room where your presentation will be made. You can prepare your poster as a series of poster panels, each of which would have been a slide in a formal oral presentation. One option is to print these poster panels and attach them directly to the poster board. Alternatively you can make a "poster sheet" containing several poster panels that is printed and attached to the poster board. The terminology used here is not universally recognized. Hence, it is important when reading this chapter to remember the definitions of the terms "poster board," "poster panel," and "poster sheet."

A distinguishing feature of a poster relative to a formal oral presentation is that everything will be seen by the audience at the same time. This means that you are somewhat restricted in the use of different backgrounds and colors for the panels. More will be said about preparing your poster in Section 5.2.

Presenting a poster differs from giving a formal oral presentation in that the audience will be standing in front of your poster rather than being seated in a room. People will be leaving and others joining continually during the poster session. Having a good audience will depend on the topic and attractiveness of your poster as well as your ability to hold their attention during your brief overview of the poster.

Although poster sessions typically last an hour or two, you will have no stipulated time limit for your overview. A poster presentation involves repeatedly giving a brief overview of the material on your poster with occasional interruptions from the audience for questions. An advantage in a poster presentation is the opportunity to have a more lengthy discussion on some aspect of your work that is of particular interest to some people in the audience. However, this needs to be done with due consideration for everyone in the audience.

A poster presentation also allows you to interact directly with your audience in order to give them your business card, a copy of a relevant paper, or to show them some object related to your presentation. You also will be speaking at the same time as other people making poster presentations in the same room. Some of these other presenters might be adjacent to where you are making your poster presentation. This introduces special considerations with respect to courtesy in giving a poster presentation.

You will be presenting your poster within a small area with limited flexibility to move around. You definitely will not be using a microphone. Since laser pointers are ineffective for poster presentations, you should use a mechanical pointer.

Owing to the more informal nature of a poster presentation, nervousness is not a major issue for most speakers. For this reason many people prefer to give a poster rather than a formal oral presentation. Note that many student technical papers competitions involve poster presentations. Hence, you want to master well all the aspects of preparing and giving an effective poster presentation!

When I need to push myself, I think of all those nicely polished trophies waiting to be lifted up by the winner - and how that winner might be me!
—Maria Sharapova, winner of 5 Grand Slam tennis titles

5.1.2 Importance of Developing Your Own Poster Presentation Style

The comment made in Chapter 4, Making a Formal Oral Presentation, that there are many ways to make a formal oral presentation also applies to giving a poster. The basic components of preparing a good presentation, namely good organization and effective visual material, must still be there. However, you have considerable latitude in developing your own poster presentation style, both with respect to preparing the poster and giving an overview of the poster material. The style you use in preparing a poster and in discussing it for the audience should evolve into a unique expression of your personality. Use your artistic talents to prepare an attractive and interesting poster. Use your showmanship to attract and engage the audience. Since the format for a poster presentation permits interacting with the audience, it provides an opportunity for you to really "turn on your personality!" This chapter gives several suggestions for preparing and giving an effective poster presentation. Incorporate the suggestions that are comfortable for you and continue to embellish your presentation style for the rest of your life!

5.2 PREPARING YOUR POSTER

5.2.1 The Plan for Laying Out Your Poster

Once your poster has been accepted for presentation, you need to start preparing it. It will take longer to prepare an effective poster presentation than to prepare a formal oral presentation. The reason for this is that you usually will generate your poster panels initially as individual slides using PowerPoint or similar utility. You can choose to print these as individual panels that you will post directly on the poster board provided at the poster session. Alternatively, you can copy several panels onto a single slide using the "Banner Mode" in PowerPoint or similar utility that you will subsequently print as a poster sheet. Printing individual panels usually requires having access to a color printer. Printing the panels on a poster sheet will require a special wide-format printer that might not be readily accessible and can be expensive. You might need to have this done by an outside vendor. Irrespective of which format you choose for posting your panels, you will need ample time to get your poster printed. Do not wait until the last minute to prepare your poster!

5.2.2 Organizing the Content of Your Poster

The organization of the panels for your poster should follow the guidelines for organizing and outlining your presentation discussed in Chapter 3, Organizing Your Presentation. The general rule for a good poster is that the content should be understandable even if you were not there to discuss it. Since in a poster presentation you do not have the luxury of using fade-in or animations, the text, figures, photographs, graphs, etc. need to be presented compactly. If space permits, consider having a relevant header for each panel such as "Overview," "Objectives," "Design Considerations," "Conclusions," etc. drawn from the major headings in your outline.

5.2.3 Designing Your Poster

When designing your poster, find out in advance how much space is allocated for posting your panels or poster sheets. Poster boards typically will accommodate panels or poster sheets that span a height of 100–130 cm (40–50 in.). The allowable width might range from just 1 m (40 in.) to as much as 2 m (80 in.) or more. If you print your poster as individual panels, you have some flexibility as to how you use the allowable poster board space. You have less flexibility if you choose to print your poster as one or more poster sheets. Poster sheets typically have a width of approximately 1 m (40 in.) owing to the limitations of commercial flat-bed printers. However, they can have a variable height. If you print your poster as one or more poster sheets, you need to make certain that the allowable poster board space will accommodate the height of your poster sheets.

Irrespective of whether you choose to post individual panels or one or more poster sheets, you need to decide whether you will use a left-to-right row or column layout. That is, will your panels be laid out from left to right horizontally in rows or vertically in columns. If for some reason you need to mix the row and column layouts, it is imperative that you number the panels or use easy-to-see arrows to indicate the flow of the material when the audience views your poster.

Be certain to use sufficiently large font size for the panels of your poster. The general rule is that anything on your poster should be easily readable from 3 m (120 in.). The same advice regarding choosing the font style for a formal oral presentation discussed in Section 4.2.3 applies to preparing your panels for a poster presentation. Avoid the more florid fonts such as Times New Roman and use the easier-to-read fonts such as Arial, Calibri (Body), Tahoma, Verdana, and others.

Choose the color scheme for your poster in view of the fact that poster sessions are always given in a well-lighted room. Color schemes that would be too harsh in a dark room might look very good for a poster presentation. In general, the color scheme for a poster should be uniform. Since the entire poster is viewed at once, changing the color scheme can be distracting for the audience. Refer to Section 4.2.5 for more discussion on choosing the color scheme for your presentation.

The title for your poster can be done as a "banner" that spans all the panels or the entire poster sheet. It also can be just one panel. Having the title span all the panels or the entire poster sheet is more likely to attract the attention of people wandering through the room in which the poster session is being held. It also makes it easier for people to find your poster if they are looking for it. The title banner or panel should include the title of your poster and the names of the coauthors and their affiliations. When there are coauthors, you should indicate in some way who you are. This can be done by underlining or highlighting your name. Include your email address and possibly your website either at the bottom of the title banner or panel, or at the bottom of the last panel on the poster sheet. Indeed, it pays to advertise!

As mentioned above, you should number each panel on your poster sheet irrespective of whether you print it as individual panels or as one more poster sheets containing multiple panels. Arrows are also an option when you have multiple panels on a poster sheet. This helps people follow the organization of the materials on your poster.

Humor can be used to make a poster more engaging. However, in contrast to a formal oral presentation in which the humor you inject might be a memorized "one-liner," humor is usually introduced visually in a poster presentation. Clip-art or cartoons can be very effective for this purpose. Since you usually will not draw any attention to the humor you inject into your poster, the connection between any clip-art or cartoon that you use should be obvious and not require any explanation from you.

5.2.4 Proofreading Your Poster Material

The same note-of-caution mentioned in Section 4.2.10 in connection with preparing the slides for a formal oral presentation applies to preparing a poster, namely to proofread your poster material very carefully. Do not trust "spell-check" and "grammar-check" utilities. If your first language is not English, have someone who is fluent in English proofread your poster material.

5.3 PRINTING YOUR POSTER

5.3.1 Choices in the Format for Printing Your Poster

Section 5.2.1 indicated that you can print your poster either as a series of individual panels or as multiple panels on one or more poster sheets. Both formats have advantages and disadvantages that will be discussed here.

Consider first printing your presentation as individual panels typically on A4 or Letter-size paper. Each of these panels would be posted individually onto the poster board provided for your poster session. This option takes more time to put up on the poster board. It also is somewhat less professional in appearance than posting one or more poster sheets having multiple panels. An advantage is that printing individual panels even in color usually can be done in-house. It also is considerably less time-consuming and less expensive than printing one or more sheets on a commercial wide-format printer. Individual panels are easy to transport in your briefcase. Another advantage is that you can made additions and corrections to the individual panels when on-site since conventional color printers are usually available either in conference business centers or in nearby copy centers. Individual panels are also convenient for making handout copies to give to interested listeners at your poster presentation.

The alternative is to print your poster as one or more sheets containing multiple panels. This is rapidly becoming the norm for poster presentations because of its professional appearance. One or more poster sheets can be put up very quickly on the poster board for your session. Rather than copying rectangular poster panels, one can use utilities such as Cinema 4D Studio and others that permit you to integrate your text, figures, and graphics in 3D directly onto a poster sheet. A disadvantage is that preparing poster sheets takes considerably more lead time. The width of the poster sheets is limited by the capability of commercial wide-format printers, which is typically approximately 1 m (40 in.). This means that the size of the panels on the poster sheet might be considerably smaller than when posting them individually. The sheets can be of any desired height if printed in the "banner mode" using PowerPoint. A typical poster height is approximately 130 cm (50 in.). If possible, print your poster as one sheet with a height compatible with the allowable space on the poster board for the session. You have the option to print your poster sheets as either glossy or laminated. The latter is recommended, since it provides protection against scratches, moisture, etc. Printing poster sheets is somewhat more expensive than printing poster panels. Printing an average size poster, 100 cm wide by 130 cm high (40 in. by 50 in.), typically will cost approximately $15–$20 (US dollars) when done "in-house" and about twice this amount when done by a commercial printing establishment. Poster sheets have some disadvantages. A poster sheet has to be transported in an appropriate "tube" to protect it from being crushed or creased. This can present a problem if you need to travel by plane to the site of the poster session. Another disadvantage of the poster sheet format is that no additions to the poster can be made on-site. In particular, any corrections cannot be made other than by inserting them by marker pen, which detracts from the appearance of the poster.

5.3.2 Proofreading Your Printed Poster

Proofread carefully to see if you any words out.

—Author unknown

Irrespective of the format you choose for printing your poster, you need to proofread the printed poster carefully. In particular, if you choose the poster sheet format, be aware that proofreading the poster prior to printing it does not ensure that the printed poster will be error-free. The reason for this is that when you created the panels for your poster you might have used special software on your computer such as MathType equation editor. You will save the electronic file created on PowerPoint or similar utility onto a storage device that you will take to some facility that has a wide-format commercial printer. This printer will be connected to a dedicated computer that probably will not have the special software that you used in preparing your poster panels. The result will be that special characters you created, e.g., by an equation editor such as MathType, might appear as completely different characters! This can be avoided by saving your PowerPoint or similar utility file in a pdf (Portable Document Format). This will prevent any special characters from being changed in the printing process.

5.4 CHECKLIST BEFORE ARRIVING ON-SITE FOR YOUR POSTER PRESENTATION

Better three hours too soon than a minute too late.
—William Shakespeare, 16th century dramatist

Before departing for the site of your poster presentation, you need to check that you have everything you need. Of course you need to take your poster presentation in either the individual panel format or the poster-sheet format. If you use the latter, you need to purchase an appropriate tube in which to carry and protect your poster sheets. These can be purchased at any office supply store and at some university bookstores. You should take along thumbtacks and removable tape to post your poster in the event that they are not provided or are not accessible when you need them. You also should bring a telescoping mechanical pointer. If you print your poster as one or more poster sheets, you should take an assortment of felt marker pens having the colors used on your poster to correct any errors or make any additions to it. Remember to bring your business cards to give to people who are interested in your poster or your qualifications. Bring any "gimmicks" (see Section 5.7.4) that you want to use to enhance your poster presentation. These might include some item related to your poster that you will pass around to the audience or a copy of a paper you have authored or coauthored that is related to your poster. You might also want to take a bottle of water to have at your poster, since you will be doing a lot of talking over a relatively long time period!

5.5 SCOPING OUT THE ROOM AND POSTING YOUR POSTER

5.5.1 Scoping Out the Room for Your Poster Presentation

Chapter 2, Preliminary Considerations, discussed things you should try to find out prior to preparing your presentation. In the case of a poster presentation, there are things that you will become aware of only after you arrive on-site. After locating the room for the poster session, you need to determine where your poster is to be posted. Poster sessions usually have assigned poster boards. Sometimes the poster session chairs will be available to direct you to where you should post your poster. Usually there will be some directive such as a page with assignments of posters to specific poster-board locations. This might be sent to you as an email communication or be available at some central point in the room where you will be giving your poster. You might be required to post your poster at some stipulated time well in advance of when the poster session begins. Clearly you should arrive sufficiently early to post your poster well before the beginning of the poster session.

5.5.2 Posting Your Poster

You need to determine if tape, thumbtacks, or other type of fastener will be provided to post your poster. Bring your own tape and thumbtacks even if the organizers indicate that they will be provided. Try to post your poster panels or poster sheets so that the midpoint of your poster is about at eye level. It is important to assess how much of the space around your poster you can reasonably use for your audience without infringing on the space of other poster presenters.

5.6 USING A MECHANICAL POINTER

5.6.1 Use a Mechanical Pointer for a Poster Presentation

They're funny things, Accidents. You never have them till you're having them.
—A. A. Milne, English author

As mentioned in Section 5.1.1, you should not use a laser pointer for a poster presentation. One reason for this is that a laser pointer is not particularly effective at the close range dictated by the format for a poster presentation. Another reason is that the audience for a poster presentation will be coming and going as well as moving about in front of your poster. A danger exists that you might flash the laser pointer in someone's eyes. Hence, you should use a mechanical pointer for a poster presentation, since they are optimal for use at short range. Since mechanical pointers are never provided for poster sessions, you must purchase your own. They can be obtained at any office supply store for just a few dollars. They are telescoping and have a clip so that they can be collapsed to the size of a ball-point pen and conveniently put it into a pocket.

5.6.2 Using a Mechanical Pointer to Control Your Audience

It might seem a bit silly to have a section on how to use a simple thing such as a mechanical pointer. However, a mechanical pointer can be used during your poster presentation to do more than just point! During a poster presentation people tend to crowd right in front of your poster, thereby obstructing the view of people in the back. A mechanical pointer can be used very effectively to control where your audience stands in front of your poster. By using a mechanical pointer as a subtle "rapier" you can move your audience into a semicircle in front of your poster to provide optimal viewing for everyone. Doing this in an inoffensive way requires a bit of practice, but is well-worth working into your poster presentation mechanics.

Ocholophobia (ok-luh-foh-bee-uh): extreme or irrational fear of or aversion to crowds.

5.6.3 Avoid "Playing" With Your Mechanical Pointer

An undesirable subconscious inclination during a poster presentation is to "play" with a mechanical pointer by telescoping it in and out. This can be distracting to your audience. It also will draw attention away from what you are trying to discuss in your poster presentation. If you are inclined to do this, it can be avoided by putting pieces of transparent tape at the joints of the telescoping mechanical pointer to prevent you from closing it during your poster presentation.

5.7 MASTERING THE MECHANICS OF AN EFFECTIVE POSTER PRESENTATION

5.7.1 Preliminary Considerations

Although a poster presentation is usually more casual than a formal oral presentation, it requires that you be much better prepared. You should be able to give a good overview of your poster in less than 5 minutes. Expect to be interrupted to answer questions during your overview. Hence, you need to know the flow of your presentation very well to enable continuing your overview after answering a question. Unfortunately using cue cards would be awkward during the many times that you will be giving your overview. However, it is helpful to prepare them anyway in the event that you have a momentary lapse-of-memory concerning some point in your overview. They also can be helpful to refresh your memory in answering questions. Since you will be repeating the overview of your poster many times over a period of an hour or more, you should have a bottle of water handy to "wet your lips."

5.7.2 Engaging Your Audience

In making a poster presentation you have fewer options for engaging your audience than in giving a formal oral presentation. For example, using a quote, adage, or poem usually will not work because you will be repeating your overview many times. However, each time you begin the overview of your poster, you could use some engaging comment such as *"This poster advances a new technology that will reduce the cost of desalinating water by 50% or more* "or" *This research uses biomimetics to produce a simple device for making potable water."* If you do choose to use some engaging opening comment for your overview, it is important that it be brief.

5.7.3 Interacting With Your Audience

Your ability to interact with your audience will be easier if they are more-or-less in a semicircle in front of your poster. As was discussed in Section 5.6.2, this can be achieved by a judicious use of a mechanical pointer.

Be careful not to give your poster to just one person when other people are present. I have judged technical poster competitions when the student presenter has recognized that I was one of the judges and subsequently catered to me to the exclusion of the other people that were interested in their poster. This was very definitely a negative in terms of my assessment of the student's handling of their poster.

It is important to bring "late arrivals" to your poster "up to speed" on where you are in your overview. If someone arrives when you are nearly at the end of your brief overview, recognize the late arrival and tell them that you are just wrapping up your overview and will provide them with an overview shortly.

Effective eye contact and body language are even more important in poster presentations because you are in close contact with your audience. Effective eye contact was discussed in some detail in Chapter 4, Making a Formal Oral Presentation. In particular, Section 4.5.3 discussed the issue of direct eye contact being a positive in Western cultures for which it conveys sincerity, but possibly being a negative factor in some non-Western cultures for which it might convey a lack of respect for someone who is senior in age or position. This issue takes on added importance when giving a poster to a global audience. The reader is advised to review what was said about eye contact in Chapter 4, Making a Formal Oral Presentation.

You will be somewhat limited in moving around when giving a poster presentation. It is important to avoid standing directly in front of your poster, since this will block the view for some people in your audience. Your options are to stand to either side of your poster. Occasionally you can casually walk from one side to the other side of your poster. In fact, it might be necessary to do this in order to use your mechanical pointer to control how the audience distributes themselves in front of your poster.

In view of the limitations in terms of engaging your audience when making a poster presentation, it is important to make effective use of body language, in particular the use of your hands. Avoid pointing to anything on your poster with your finger or your hand, since this will require you to move in front of some parts of your poster. Use a mechanical pointer to draw attention to the material on your poster.

5.7.4 "Gimmicks" for Making an Effective Poster Presentation

Become so wrapped up in something that you forget to be afraid!
—Lady Bird Johnson, wife of US President Lyndon Johnson

The fact that you can interact with your audience during a poster presentation provides an opportunity to use "gimmicks" to make it more effective. For example, you might bring a sample of something related to the subject of your poster that you can pass around to the audience. This could be a microchip, a hollow fiber membrane, samples of "before" and "after" such as a small vile of a dirty water feed and a vile of clean water permeate from some water-treatment technology, etc.

It is also effective to include a "pocket" on your poster board that contains hard copies of the paper on which your poster is based. Invite your audience to take a copy of this paper. A "pocket" can also be used to contain a page that lists the title of your poster, the coauthors, their affiliations, an abstract of your poster, and a list of publications of your research group that are relevant to the topic of your poster.

You also can give your audience something to take home with them such as a pen with your university logo on it, an LCD screen wiper, etc. Again, it pays to advertise!

You definitely should include a "pocket" or small box affixed to your poster board that contains your business cards. This saves you from being interrupted during your overview by people requesting your business card. Moreover, it is a very professional way to handle making your business card available to your audience.

5.8 POSTER SESSION COURTESY

5.8.1 Courtesy Considerations for Poster Presentations

Poster sessions involve many posters being presented simultaneously, sometimes as many as 50 or more. You will be in close contact with your audience and in close proximity to other people making poster presentations. For these reasons the issue of courtesy deserves special attention both with respect to its implications for your audience and for the other speakers presenting posters.

5.8.2 Courtesy Considerations Regarding Your Audience

Respect for your audience means that you should be at your poster throughout the times for your session. Since people typically want to view several posters at a poster session, they need to visit the posters of interest to them in a timely manner. It is disrespectful to people interested in your poster if you are not at your poster when they stop by to view it. In particular, if you are in a technical papers poster competition and not at your poster when a judge stops to view it, you will jeopardize your chances of receiving an award! If you do need to leave your poster for some reason (e.g., a bathroom break),

66 Presenting an Effective and Dynamic Technical Paper

you should leave a prominent note on your poster indicating the time when you left the poster and the time when you will be back.

As mentioned in Section 5.1.1, poster sessions are usually quite casual. Questions are not deferred to the end of your overview. It is courteous to invite your audience to ask questions anytime during your overview of the poster. As discussed in Section 4.6.5, you should always thank any person who asks a question and extend some brief compliment to them for asking the question. If you have a large audience for your poster or if the room is noisy, you should repeat the question so that everyone in your audience can hear it.

If you bring people to tears with your words, consider the possibility that you have really bad breath!

—Author unknown

A significant difference in giving a poster is that you are in close contact with your audience. Hence, you must be careful about what you eat before you give your poster. In particular, onions, garlic, coffee, beer, wine, etc. can give you an objectionable bad breath that could cost you an award! You might want to bring some breath mints in the event that you do develop halitosis (bad breath!). Being a bit nervous could cause you to perspire a bit in which case BO (Body Odor) could become a problem. Hence, men should consider using an after-shave lotion or cologne and women a nice perfume to combat any offensive BO. Sometimes poster sessions involve hors de oeuvres and beverages. Be careful not to talk when you are eating or drinking. It is better to avoid eating or drinking anything other than an occasional swig of water during your poster presentation.

Poster session courtesy includes welcoming the people who come to your poster and thanking those who stayed for your overview. Encourage people to take one of your business cards before they leave if you have included some provision for this. Ask anyone who showed a particular interest in your poster for their business card.

5.8.3 Courtesy Considerations Regarding Other Poster Presenters

Since poster sessions involve simultaneous presentations, be aware of the poster presenters adjacent to you. Make certain that your audience does not "spill over" into the space of those presenting posters next to you. Be careful not to speak too loudly such that you "drown-out" the presenters next to you, particularly if you are a man with a strong, deep voice.

5.9 DEVELOPING YOUR POSTER PRESENTATION STYLE

Developing your style in giving a poster is an evolutionary process just as it is in making a formal oral presentation. However, since the forum for giving a poster is usually casual, chances are that you will develop your poster style more rapidly than your formal oral presentation style. Indeed, a more relaxed atmosphere is far more conducive for bringing out your public-speaking abilities. Pick and choose among the elements for enhancing your poster presentation that you are most comfortable in using.

One of the best ways to improve your poster style is to reverse-engineer effective poster presentations that you attend. Try to assess what features of an effective poster presentation really engaged your attention and made you want to learn more about the topic of the poster. Observe how experienced poster presenters handle distributing their audience around their poster and how they address the inevitable interruptions for questions from the audience. A natural progression in developing your public-speaking ability is to move from being somewhat afraid to speak in public to looking forward to opportunities to present your work to an audience. However, in developing your public-speaking abilities you are never "there" in terms of arriving at some pinnacle of effectiveness. Irrespective of how accomplished you are or how effective you become at public speaking, you will continue to improve for the rest of your professional life!

NOTES

Appendix A

Quick Reference Guide for Giving a Formal Oral Presentation

- Have you checked on the venue and time allocation?
- Have you outlined your presentation according to the guidelines in Chapter 3, Organizing Your Presentation?
- Have you prepared compact cue-cards for your presentation?
- Have you prepared your slides according to the guidelines in Chapter 4, Making a Formal Oral Presentation?
- Have you numbered your slides?
- Have you carefully proofread your presentation?
- Have you practiced giving your presentation within the stipulated time limit?
- Have you determined if you speak at a podium or will be free to move about?
- Have you determined if a microphone will be available and if so what type it will be?
- Is your planned attire appropriate for the occasion and will it accommodate the microphone and transmitter?
- Do you have a laser remote and did you bring extra batteries?
- Do you know how to pronounce the name of the person who will introduce you?
- If your name is difficult to pronounce, have you prepared a card with your name phonetically spelled to give to the session chair, cochair, or host?
- Have you prepared a few "one-liners" to inject in the event that you have a momentary lapse-of-memory?
- Have you arranged with one or more people who will be in the audience some means of communication if you want to defer questions to them that you cannot answer?
- Do you have business cards to give to people after your presentation?

Appendix B

Quick Reference Guide for Making a Poster Presentation

- Have you checked on the space allocated for your poster?
- Have you outlined your presentation according to the guidelines in Chapter 3, Organizing Your Presentation?
- Have you prepared cue cards to help you remember the flow of your short overview?
- Have you prepared your poster according to the guidelines in Chapter 5, Giving a Poster Presentation?
- Have you carefully proofread your printed poster?
- Do you have appropriate materials for posting your poster?
- Do you have a mechanical pointer?
- Have you practiced giving an overview of your poster in 3–5 minutes?
- Have you planned for any "gimmicks" to enhance your poster such as discussed in Chapter 5, Giving a Poster Presentation?
- Do you have business cards to give to people?

Appendix C

Typical Criteria for Judging a Poster Competition

TECHNICAL:

Content (30 points): Thoroughness and quality of material; important and relevant items included and presented in the poster:

- ✓ Appropriate introduction
- ✓ Review of prior relevant studies
- ✓ Statement of objectives
- ✓ Technical approach/methodology
- ✓ Outcome—results of research project
- ✓ Discussion of technical challenges
- ✓ Presentation of meaningful results
- ✓ Significant conclusions
- ✓ Some assessment of reproducibility and experimental error

Comprehension (30 points):

- ✓ Demonstrated the ability to interact with the reviewers by answering questions and providing clear explanations
- ✓ Showed understanding of the importance of the research work
- ✓ Demonstrated the ability to relate relevance of the work to the larger picture or research issue, thereby realizing the significance of his/her results
- ✓ Provided well thought-out suggestions for future work

NONTECHNICAL:

Organization of Poster (20 points): Contains all the necessary components of an effective poster

- ✓ Descriptive title
- ✓ Authors

- ✓ Effective introduction
- ✓ Clear statement of objectives
- ✓ Review of prior studies
- ✓ Sound research plan
- ✓ Indication of the major challenges that needed to be addressed
- ✓ Effective presentation of results
- ✓ Presentation of succinct major conclusions
- ✓ Appropriate acknowledgments

Presentation of Poster (20 points):

- ✓ Good eye contact and vocalization of the presenter
- ✓ Professional appearance of the presenter
- ✓ Enthusiasm of the presenter, showing the ability to address and involve all attendees of the poster session
- ✓ Effective use of pointer
- ✓ Effective use of color, figures, graphs, tables
- ✓ Use of appropriate font size
- ✓ Self-explanatory graphs and figures
- ✓ Indication of reproducibility of data

Appendix D

Considerations When Critiquing a Presentation

This is a template for "reverse-engineering" a presentation that you hear. It is divided into considerations related to the organization of the talk and those related to the presentation style of the speaker. Under each element of the organization and style, questions are posed to help you assess the effectiveness of the presentation. It is helpful to use a copy of this critique that has the questions below each heading omitted so that you can write brief notes regarding how a speaker addressed each of the elements in their presentation.

ORGANIZATION

Title Slide:
    Did the speaker thank the person who introduced them by name?
    Did the speaker repeat any information already given by the person who introduced them?
    Did the speaker mention any information on the title slide not given when they were introduced (e.g., coauthors)?
    Did the title describe the presentation well and was it brief?
    Did the speaker define any acronyms or abbreviations that appeared in the title?
    Did the speaker mention that their slides were numbered?

Overview Slide:
    Did the overview slide provide a good "roadmap" of the talk?
    Did the overview slide include the words "objectives" and "conclusions"?

Introduction:
    Did the speaker use some interesting facts, figures, or visuals to generate interest in the topic?
    Did the introduction effectively lead to the focus of the talk?

Review of Prior Studies:
  Did the speaker include some review of prior studies?
  How did the speaker choose to organize the review of prior studies?
  Did the review of prior studies lead to the challenges in the field?
  Did the review of prior studies lead to the objectives of the work?
  Did the speaker have a separate slide or panel in which the objectives were succinctly stated?
Research Plan:
  Did the speaker mention the design considerations required to achieve the objectives?
  Did the speaker have a research plan that summarized how the problem was tackled?
Research Results:
  How were the results presented (e.g., figures, graphs, micrographs, photographs, etc.)
  Did the speaker provide some measure of the error in data that were presented (e.g., replicates, remeasurements, regression coefficient, standard error, t-test, etc.)?
  Were data shown as points and theoretical or model predictions shown as continuous lines?
  Was the number of equations in a modeling or theoretical study appropriate?
  Were all the symbols and the underlying physics in the equations described?
Discussion of Results:
  Did the speaker adequately explain their results?
  Did the speaker emphasize the novelty and significance of their results?
Conclusions:
  Did the conclusions relate back to the stated objectives?
  Were the conclusions stated concisely?
Acknowledgments and Thank You:
  Did the speaker include acknowledgments and Thank You slides?
  Did the speaker include their email address and web site?

STYLE

Quality of the Visuals (color scheme, size of font, etc.):
  Was the font sufficiently large to be read from the most distant point in the room?
  Was the color scheme attractive and easy on the eyes?
  Did the speaker use a template and if so did it interfere with any text or figures?
  Were there any typographical or grammatical errors?

Were all acronyms and abbreviations defined on the visuals?

Speaker Qualities (appearance, voice projection, eye contact, body language, etc.):

Was the speaker's eye contact good to all points in the room?

If possible, did the speaker move around a bit to facilitate eye contact?

Did the speaker use voice inflection and the pause to make the talk more engaging?

Did the speaker speak to the screen or to the audience?

Did the speaker read the text on the visuals or paraphrase it?

Was the speaker aware of where to stand to avoid blocking the view of anyone?

Did the speaker smile occasionally to establish better rapport with the audience?

Was the speaking pace appropriate to permit understanding the speaker?

Did the speaker express excitement when discussing significant results?

Did the speaker encounter any problems (e.g., lapse-of-memory, equipment malfunction, etc.) and did they handle them well?

Effectiveness (techniques for generating interest in his/her topic):

How did the speaker begin their presentation to generate interest?

Did the speaker provide any interesting facts, figures, or visuals to generate interest?

Did the speaker use any rhetorical questions to generate interest?

Did the speaker refer to anything said by a speaker in an earlier presentation?

Did the speaker use body language well such as effective use of the hands?

Did the speaker have any distracting mannerisms (e.g., pacing, slouching, swinging their arms, hands in their pockets, chewing, etc.)?

Pace of the Presentation (allocation of time):

Did the speaker get to their stated objectives within one-fourth or one-third of the way into the allotted time for their presentation?

Was the time allocated by the speaker for the various parts of their presentation (i.e., introduction, prior studies, research plan, discussion, and conclusions) appropriate?

Was the presentation well-paced or did it appear that the speaker was rushed during their discussion of results and conclusions?

Did the speaker finish in time to entertain questions?

Pointer Use:

Did the speaker hold the pointer steady and avoid waving it?

Did the speaker use the pointer effectively to draw your attention to particular text or visuals?

Did the speaker avoid pointing with their arm or finger?

Use of Humor, Animations, and Sounds:
  Did the speaker inject any humor?
  Did the speaker use any animations such as to show the operation of their apparatus?
  Did the speaker change the color of the font or background to emphasize any of their visuals?
  Did the speaker use any sounds and if so were they effective?

Appendix E

Web Sites for Outstanding Presentations

I have chosen to give you the URLs for presentations made by four outstanding speakers. I have chosen these four speakers for reasons that will become clear to you from my overview of each video and by viewing them. In the following, the speakers are listed alphabetically. I provide an overview of each video presentation in which I highlight some of the aspects of public speaking that it demonstrates very well. As mentioned in Section 4.8, Practice Makes Perfect no one is perfect. This also applies to anyone giving a presentation. Hence, I also point out in my overview some things in the presentations of each of these outstanding speakers that could be improved.

A wonderful source of public-speaking videos is the TED (Technology, Entertainment, and Design) website at https://www.ted.com/. In 1984 TED was established as a nonprofit organization with a focus on sponsoring conferences to spread ideas, particularly in the form of short talks (usually 18 minutes or less). It covers a broad spectrum of topics including science, business, and global issues. All four outstanding speakers featured here have video presentations on TED. You are strongly urged to explore the TED website to view more videos of public speaking!

AL GORE

Al Gore is an American politician and environmentalist. He was elected to both the US House of Representatives and the US Senate. From 1993 to 2001 he served as the 45th Vice President of the United States under President Bill Clinton. In addition to serving on the Board of Directors for Apple Inc., he is the cofounder and Chairman of Generation Investment Management and is a senior partner at Kleiner, Perkins, Caufield and Byers. His principal focus today is serving as Chairman of the Climate Reality

Project, a nonprofit organization devoted to solving the climate crisis. Al Gore is a very effective and entertaining public speaker. He can be viewed at the following URL:

https://www.ted.com/talks/al_gore_s_new_thinking_on_the_climate_crisis

This is a video of a 27-minute presentation that Al Gore made in 2008 at the Naval Post-Graduate Laboratory in Monterey, California. This is a technical talk on global climate change. Al Gore begins his presentation using a meaningful quote from Mahatma Gandhi and very quickly moves into the body of his presentation. His slides are particularly attractive and were prepared with a different utility than PowerPoint. He uses a laser pointer although this is difficult to see in the video. The font that he uses for all his slides is very easy-to-read. He uses fade-in to handle more complex slides. Color is used for emphasis on some of his slides. For example, he uses green for words related to the environment and red for words encouraging action. Effective comparisons are used to underscore the impact of global climate change. For example, he shows the shrinking of the polar ice cap in comparison to comparable land area in the U.S. He also introduces humor at a few points in his talk. For example, he has a cartoon that illustrates how many tons of carbon dioxide we are pouring into the atmosphere each year by having an equivalent number of cartoon-type elephants in the sky. Al Gore's talk does have a few deficiencies. He dresses a bit casual for an audience that has mid- and high-level management people including several that serve on the boards of major companies. He also puts his left hand into the pocket of his trousers a few times, which does not project a positive image. He also does not consistently define the axes in the graphs that he presents. He entertains two questions at the end of his talk, but is a bit "long-winded" in answering them.

DEL HARVEY

Del Harvey is Vice President for Trust and Safety at Twitter. In this capacity she heads up Twitter's antispam effort to eliminate threats such as "phishing" and hacking. Del Harvey has an unusual background for someone with so much power over public speech. She is not a lawyer and will not even say if she graduated from college. Her education about the dark side of the Internet came instead from experience. In 2003, when she was 21, she started volunteering for Perverted Justice, a group that posed as young kids online to engage potential pedophiles in chats. She is exceptionally effective at public speaking as you will see from the following URL:

https://www.ted.com/talks/del_harvey_the_strangeness_of_scale_at_twitter

This is a presentation made by Del Harvey in 2014. She is dressed smartly and appropriately for her audience. She begins her presentation with some startling facts about spam on the Internet that immediately command your attention. Her slides are very effective. Fade-in is used to avoid having the audience read her slides before she discusses them. When she presents graphs, she defines the axes before discussing them. Del Harvey asks quite a few rhetorical questions during this talk to establish rapport with her audience. She always pauses for a few seconds after each rhetorical question to give the audience a little time to think about the answer. Although she does not move around on the stage for her presentation, she has excellent body language. She turns to each side to encompass the entire audience. Del Harvey has particularly expressive eyes and she uses them well—her eye contact with the audience is excellent! She also uses her hands very effectively to complement what she is saying. She has no annoying or distracting mannerisms. One thing that would have improved Del Harvey's presentation would have been to number her slides to permit people to refer to them during questions after her presentation.

DR. HANS ROSLING

Hans Rosling is a Swedish medical doctor, academician, statistician, and public speaker. He is currently a Professor of International Health at the Karolinska Institutet in Sweden. He was instrumental in developing the Trendalyzer software system that converts international statistics into moving, interactive graphics. This software system was acquired by Google in 2007. He rose to international celebrity status after presenting a TED Talk in which he promoted the use of data to explore development issues. In 2012 he was named by *Time* magazine among the 100 most influential people in the world.

Hans Rosling is an excellent role model for speakers whose first language is not English. In fact, he speaks English with a rather heavy Swedish accent. However, he is such an effective public speaker that his accent is not at all distracting. He gives his presentations with a very serious demeanor, but has a very clever way of introducing humor into his presentations. The URLs for two Hans Rosling talks are included here:

http://www.gapminder.org/videos/gapmindervideos/gapcast-1-health-money-sex-in-sweden/

https://www.youtube.com/watch?v=YpKbO6O3O3M

The first video is approximately 7 minutes long and involves just one slide. This presentation was prepared in 2004 using the Trendalyzer software developed by Hans Rosling's Gapminder Foundation in Sweden. However, this one slide conveys much information via Hans Rosling's extensive use of fade-in and animations. Effective components of public speaking to notice in this presentation are Hans Rosling's use of voice inflection, the rhetorical question, body language, in particular the use of his hands, and subtle humor. Hans Rosling also knows the flow of his talk very well—he always knows what will be on the screen before it appears.

Note that he begins his talk by showing a graph for which he immediately defines the axes. Some elements of Hans Rosling's presentation style do not follow the recommendations of this guidebook. For example, his attire is casual for a formal oral presentation. He also points with his arm rather than using a laser or mechanical pointer. He can "get away" with these departures from good practice because he is a world-class figure in both science and public speaking.

The second video is approximately 19 minutes long. It was made in 2007 and also uses the Trendalyzer software. The subject of this second video is Hans Rosling's analysis of world poverty. His major point is that lifting all peoples of this world out of poverty, which some people consider to be impossible, in fact it is possible. In order to demonstrate that the impossible is possible, at approximately 17 minutes into this talk, Hans Rosling takes off his clothes to reveal a superhero suit and proceeds to swallow a sword! His presentation style in this talk is also unconventional by the standards of this guidebook. His attire is very casual, he points with his arm, and occasionally puts his hand into a pocket in his trousers. Nonetheless, listening and watching Hans Rosling give a talk is spellbinding!

JOE WONG

Joe Wong is a Chinese-American comedian and biochemist. He was born in 1970 to a Korean-Chinese family in China. He graduated from Jilin University and the Chinese Academy of Sciences. In 1994 he entered Rice University in Texas where he received a PhD in biochemistry. He moved to Boston in 2001 and began to perform comedy at the All Asia Bar at Stash's Comedy Jam. He attracted nationwide attention after appearing in 2009 on the Late Show with David Letterman. In 2010 he placed first in the Third Annual Great American Comedy Festival. In 2013 he moved back to China, where he is now hosting shows on China Central Television. Joe Wong is an excellent role model for aspiring Asian speakers. In particular, he demonstrates very convincingly that Asians can be very good at introducing humor into their presentations! Check out Joe Wong at the following URL:

https://www.youtube.com/watch?v=buSv1jjAels&feature=youtu.be

This video is a 5-minute talk given by Joe Wong at the annual American Radio and Television Correspondents' Dinner in 2010. This was a celebrity event that included attendees such as Joe Biden, Vice President of the United States. It is a nontechnical talk that involves almost continuous humorous "one-liners." Joe Wong's humor is delightfully funny and is never offensive in any way. He demonstrates all the qualities of effective public speaking. He is typical of speakers from Chinese cultures in that he is wearing a dress suit and tie. Indeed, he is appropriately dressed to give a formal oral presentation for this auspicious occasion. He uses encompassing eye contact, employs his hands for emphasis, smiles occasionally without laughing at his own jokes, asks rhetorical questions, and uses the pause very well. He speaks English with an accent. However, this in no way detracts from his very effective speaking style. He demonstrates that speakers coming from non-Western cultures can use humor in a very entertaining way!

Appendix F

Overview of Online Materials

The online materials can be found at the following URL:
http://booksite.elsevier.com/9780128054185
These materials include the following:

- An outline prepared for the digital recording of PowerPoint presentation #1 by the author.
- Cue cards prepared for the digital recording of PowerPoint presentation #1 by the author. Note that the cue cards have 19 headings corresponding to each of the 19 slides in this presentation. However, the information in the cue cards is quite different from that in the outline for the presentation. Whereas the outline is used to prepare the presentation, the cue cards contain information deemed important in giving the presentation.
- PowerPoint presentation #1 that was given at an international technical meeting in 2006. This presentation had 19 slides for a 20-minute talk with an additional 5 minutes for questions. The slides are numbered in the header beginning with the overview slide. The title slide includes the names and affiliations of the coauthors along with the venue, date of the presentation, and the logos for the universities of the coauthors. The overview (outline) includes the words "objectives" and "conclusions." Acronyms introduced in the overview (and elsewhere in the presentation) are defined at the bottom of the slide. The introduction is covered in four slides that lead to the technological barrier (challenge) for which the background color is subtly changed from blue to black. The three objectives of this study then are defined. Prior studies are reviewed chronologically in one slide with the bibliographic citations given in smaller font at the bottom of the slide. The experiment design, methodology, and conditions are covered in five slides. The first of these includes an animation of ultrasonic time-domain reflectometry (UTDR) that shows the operating principle far more effectively than a photograph. The results are summarized in two slides that include graphs and scanning electron microscopy (SEM) images. Prominent scale bars are inserted, since those generated on the micrographs by the SEM software are not easily seen.

Five conclusions are summarized, three of which relate back to the stated objectives and two of which relate to unexpected significant results that emanated from this study. The "Thank You" slide ends the presentation on a "lighter" note showing a caricature of the author that invites questions and gives the author's email address. Clip-art humor is inserted on several slides in this presentation.

- A digital recording of the author giving PowerPoint presentation #1 as part of an oral communication skills workshop that he gave at the National Taiwan University in 2011. The author interrupts himself during this presentation to point out how he is using the various techniques for enhancing a talk that are discussed in this guidebook.
- PowerPoint presentation #2 that was given by the author as a keynote address at a technical meeting in 2016. This involved 35 slides for a 35-minute talk followed by 5 minutes for questions. The slides are numbered in the lower right-hand corner. Animation is used for a blinking circle around the slide number on the title slide. This served to remind the author to mention to the audience that the slides are numbered in the event that they want to ask a question on a particular slide. The title slide includes the names and affiliations of the coauthors along with the venue, date of the presentation, and the logos for the university, research center, and that of the organization for which the presentation was being given. This talk uses animation for a provocative opening that involves four slides that underscore the importance of "Thinking Outside the Box." The introduction constitutes nine slides that lead to the objectives of this research (slide 15). The experiment design, methodology, and results are divided into those relating to the morphology of the cryogels developed in this study and those relating to the biocidal activity of these cryogels. The methodology for characterizing the cryogel morphology is covered in one slide. The corresponding results for the cryogel morphology are covered in seven slides that include three digital recordings that very effectively illustrate the properties of the novel materials developed in this study. The methodology for characterizing the biocidal efficacy of these cryogels is summarized in one slide. The results for the biocidal properties of the cryogels developed in this study are covered in five slides. The seven conclusions in slide 32 relate back to the objectives defined in slide 15. A touch of humor is added via clip-art and a cartoon at the end that relates to the subject of the talk. An integrating feature of this talk is that the concepts of "Thinking Outside the Box" and "Food for Thought," which are introduced at the beginning of the presentation in slides 2 and 3, are reintroduced at the end of the talk in slides 32 and 33 to tie things together. The "Thank You" slide ends on a "light note" by showing a comical caricature of the author inviting questions and giving his email address. Animation and fade-in are used for the more complex slides throughout the presentation.

- Poster presentation #1 that was prepared using PowerPoint. This constitutes 18 panels that were printed as two poster sheets, each of which had nine panels. These two poster sheets would be attached to the poster board such that the right edge of the left poster sheet would mate with the left edge of the right poster sheet along the blue line in the middle of this poster. This illustrates one way to address the finite width limitation of commercial wide-format printers. This poster is shown in the online materials as it would have been posted on the poster board. The title for each poster panel is preceded by the panel number. In addition, a small "hand" directs the viewer to the next panel. The title of the poster along with the names and affiliations of the coauthors are shown in the banner mode that spans the entire width of the poster. The color theme for the poster panels is consistent and uses the colors (blue, orange, and white) of the National University of Singapore with whom the author was affiliated. Clip-art humor is used subtly on several of the poster panels. This poster did not involve presenting any research results, but rather discussed a pedagogical tool. Hence, this presentation did not involve any research objectives or conclusions. In lieu of conclusions, the presentation includes a summary poster panel. The poster board had a pocket containing copies of one of the author's papers on the subject of this poster and a small box containing business cards of the author that the audience could take.
- A digital recording of the author giving poster presentation #1 as part of an oral communication skills workshop that he gave at the National University of Singapore in 2007. The author interrupts himself during his informal poster presentation to point out how he is using the various techniques for enhancing a talk that are discussed in this guidebook. The author challenged the workshop students to make giving this poster difficult for him. This meant that they should try to crowd around the poster. The author effected "crowd control" by using his mechanical pointer to position his audience around the poster. The author also encouraged the workshop students to come up to his poster as well as to leave while he was giving his brief overview. This was to show how he handled bringing new people into his audience and thanking those who were leaving for attending his poster. This digital recording also includes the lengthy discussion period after the author's poster presentation during which the students asked interesting questions related to preparing and giving a poster presentation. Since the students were somewhat distant from the location of the acoustic pick-up for the digital recording, it is difficult to hear their questions. However, the nature of their questions is clear from the author's response to them.

- Poster presentation #2 that was prepared using Cinema 4D Studio. This powerful software permits preparing poster sheets integrating text, figures, and graphics seamlessly. This poster involves six panels that are laid out in a column format rather than the row format used in poster presentation #1. The title for each poster panel is preceded by the panel number. The title for the poster along with the names and affiliations of the coauthors are in a banner that spans the width of the poster sheet. The introduction constitutes panels 1 and 2. Two objectives are defined in panel 3. The experiment design is given in panel 4. The results and discussion are summarized in panel 5 for which the column format works well to accommodate its longer vertical dimension. Five conclusions are summarized in panel 6 that relate back to the objectives. The references and logos appear in the banner mode at the bottom of the poster.

Index

A

Abstract
  content of, 16–17
  organization of, 16–17
  when to include, 16
  word count limit, 16–17
Accent. *See* Vocalization
Acknowledgments
  what to include, 24
  whom to include, 24
Acronyms
  defining, 19, 31–32
Animation
  fade-in for text, figures and graphs, 29–30, 56
  to indicate slide number, 18, 33, 43
  to replace photo of apparatus, 20, 32
  use of, 31–32
Attire. *See* Dressing for the occasion
Audience
  awareness of during formal oral presentation, 11, 29, 37, 42
  awareness of during poster presentation, 53–55, 63–64
  communicating to, 31–32, 38–39
  controlling during poster presentation, 62, 64
  eye contact with, 38–39, 64
  handling questions, 24, 47, 63, 66
  motivating, 1–2, 18, 27, 43–44
Audio-visual equipment
  checking in advance of presentation, 8–9, 34–35
  laser pointer. *See* Laser pointer
  microphone. *See* Microphone
  projector. *See* Projectors

B

Body language. *See* Style
Business cards
  use after formal oral presentation, 47
  use during poster presentation, 54, 60, 65, 67, 69, 71

C

Clip-art
  use of, 24–25, 41, 46, 57
Coauthors
  format for listing, 2, 17–18, 24, 43, 57, 65
  multicultural considerations, 2, 17
Conclusions
  format for stating, 23
  relating back to objectives, 23, 27
Considerations
  in making a presentation, 2, 7, 19, 21–22
  preliminary to making a presentation, 7, 28, 33, 60, 63, 65–67
Courtesy
  coughing or sneezing, 35
  eating and drinking during poster presentation, 66
  helping session chair pronounce your name, 43, 69
  repeating a question from the audience, 47, 66
  special considerations during poster presentation, 54, 65–67
  thanking audience after formal oral presentation, 34–35, 46–47
  thanking session chairs and session organizers, 43, 47
  when you need to leave your poster presentation, 65–66

89

Critiquing. *See* Formal oral presentation; Poster presentation
Cue cards
 content, 10–11
 how to use, 10–11, 42
 including opener for your talk, 45
 information to include on, 10–11, 45
 sample for formal oral presentation, 85

D
Delivery
 style. *See* Style
Discussion of results
 emphasizing interesting and significant, 22–24
 labeling axes on graphs, 22, 80–82
 presenting data, 22
 presenting theoretical results, 21–22
 providing scale for micrographs and photographs, 22
 showing measure of error or reproducibility, 22–23, 73
 ways to present, 22
Dressing for the occasion
 allowing for microphone. *See* Microphone
 dress codes, 11–13
 importance of, 11–12
 making positive impression, 11
 multicultural considerations, 11–13
 recommendations, 11–13, 80, 82
 special considerations for women, 12–13
 using lanyard for clip-on microphone, 12–13
 venue considerations, 11–12
 wearing ethnic dress, 12–13

E
Equations
 defining symbols in, 21–22
 minimizing number of, 21–22
 use of block diagram for presenting, 21–22
Experimental error
 remeasurement, 22–23
 replication, 22–23
 ways to indicate, 22–23
Eye contact
 during formal oral presentation, 38–39, 77
 during poster presentation, 64
 multicultural considerations, 38–39
 techniques for effective, 38–39

F
Figures
 font size for, 30–32, 56, 76
 preparing, 22
Focus
 of this guidebook, 1–2
Font
 changing for emphasis, 31
 changing size to define acronyms, 31–32
 changing size to emphasize an equation, 31–32
 choice of color, 30–32
 choice of size, 30, 56
 choice of type, 29–30
Formal oral presentation
 choosing template for slides. *See* Slides
 chronological progression through, 19
 citing coauthors in title. *See* Coauthors
 color scheme for slides. *See* Slides
 critiquing, 51, 67, 75–78
 developing your own style. *See* Style
 digitally recording for practice, 50–51
 digital recording of, 40, 50–51
 distinguishing features of, 27–28
 ending, 46–47
 engaging your audience. *See* Generating interest
 examples of, 85–86
 format for conclusions. *See* Conclusions
 format for objectives. *See* Objectives
 generating interest. *See* Generating interest
 giving, 3, 11–13, 27, 69–70
 handling memory lapse. *See* Memory lapse
 handling mistakes. *See* Mistakes
 handling nervousness. *See* Nervousness
 handling questions. *See* Questions
 helping with pronouncing your name, 43, 69
 injecting humor. *See* Generating interest
 organization. *See* Organization
 outline or overview. *See* Outline
 practicing, 50–51
 preparation before, 8–13
 preparation on-site, 33–35
 preparing slides. *See* Slides
 prior studies. *See* Prior studies
 results. *See* Presentation
 showing figures. *See* Figures
 showing graphs. *See* Graphs
 showing micrographs. *See* Micrographs
 slides. *See* Slides

Index   91

things to check out when arriving on-site, 33–35
time allocation, 9, 45–46
use of laser pointer. *See* Laser pointer
using provocative images. *See* Generating interest
using quips. *See* Generating interest
using quotes. *See* Generating interest
ways to improve, 51
your introduction as the speaker, 43
Format
  for citing coauthors. *See* Coauthors
  for conclusions. *See* Conclusions
  for objectives. *See* Objectives
  formal oral versus poster presentation, 3, 27–28, 53–54
Future work
  when to include, 24

G

Generating interest
  creating electronic file of materials for, 41, 45
  via opening rhetorical question, 44
  via opening with a provocative image, 45
  via opening with a provocative statement, 43–44
  via opening with a quote, 44–45
  via opening with humor, 44–45
Gimmicks
  box for business cards, 65
  copy of poster presentation, 64–65
  copy of related publications, 65
  for enhancing poster presentation, 64–65, 71
  item for audience to take home, 65
  item to pass around audience, 60, 65
Graphs
  defining axes, 80–82
  lines through data points of, 22
  preparing, 22
Guidebook
  focus of, 1–2
  how to use, 4
  organization of, 3
  scope of, 1–2

H

Humor
  creating electronic file of material for, 41, 45
  introducing in slides, 41
  introducing using clip art, 41, 46, 57
  introducing verbally, 41
  multicultural considerations, 40–41
  'one-liners' for handling mistakes, 49–50
  things to avoid, 40–41
  use of, 40–41
  ways to include, 40–41

I

Introduction
  content, 19
  defining acronyms and abbreviations, 19, 75
  to this guidebook, 1–2
  indicating technological challenges, 1–2, 75
  organization of leading to objectives, 19, 75
  purpose in organizing presentation, 19
  starting dynamically. *See* Generating interest
  your introduction as the speaker. *See* Formal oral presentation

L

Language. *See* Multicultural
Laser pointer
  advice for purchasing, 36
  avoiding shaking it, 49, 77
  carrying extra batteries, 36, 69
  desirable features, 36
  green versus red, 36
  remote for advancing slides, 35–36
  using, 35–36, 69
  when to use, 36, 54, 61–62

M

Mechanical pointer
  to control distribution of audience around poster, 62–63, 87
  using, 61–63
  when to use, 54, 60–62
Memory lapse
  avoiding awkward interjections, 42
  handling, 10–11, 41–42
  opportunity to introduce humor, 42, 49–50
  using a memorized quip, 42
  value of cue cards, 10–11, 42, 45, 77
Micrographs
  preparing, 22
  showing length scale, 22, 87

Microphone
    clipped to your apparel, 12–13, 43
    directionality of fixed, 35
    handling transmitter, 12–13, 40, 69
    locating clip-on type, 12, 34
    optimal distance from, 13, 35
    at the podium, 34–35
    special considerations for women, 12–13, 43, 54
    when to use, 35, 37, 54
Mistakes
    being prepared to handle, 41, 49–50
    handling, 41, 49–50
    opportunity to introduce humor, 41, 49–50
    using quips for handling, 41, 49–50
Motivating the audience. *See also* Generating interest
    via dramatic images, 45, 77
    via facts and figures, 45, 77
    via humor, 44–45
    via quotation, 45
Multicultural
    as it relates to the speaker, 2
    as its relates to the audience, 2, 37–39
    considerations, 2, 11–13, 17, 37–39
    English not first language, 2, 11, 30, 33, 37–38, 48, 57
    ethnic attire. *See* Dressing for the occasion
    how to handle eye contact. *See* Eye contact
    how to use humor. *See* Humor
    presentations in countries other than your own. *See* Humor

N

Nervousness
    aggravated by what you eat or drink, 49, 66
    avoiding by practicing public speaking, 50
    cause of, 49–50
    channeling it into projecting excitement, 48–49
    controlling, 48–50
    gaining confidence by effective opening, 49
    loosening up by asking questions of earlier speakers, 49
    loosening up by introducing humor, 49
    memorizing beginning of your talk, 45
    shaking laser pointer, 49
    undue concern regarding accent, 37–38
    use of the smile, 49
Numbering slides. *See* Slides

O

Objectives
    conclusions relating back to, 23, 76
    format for stating, 16–17, 19
    importance of stating, 9–10, 19–20, 76
    time at which stated in presentation, 45–46, 77
On-line materials
    digital recording of poster presentation, 87
    digital recording of PowerPoint presentation, 85–86
    sample cue cards for formal oral presentation, 85
    sample formal oral presentation, 86–87
    sample outline of formal oral presentation, 85
    sample poster presentation as poster panels, 87
    sample poster presentation as poster sheet, 88
Organization
    of a technical talk, 1–2, 15
    template for, 1–2
    of this guidebook, 1–2
Outline
    bulleted list for overview of presentation, 18–19
    importance for presentation, 9–10
    indicating where slides or poster panels will be used, 9–10
    major sections for a presentation, 9–10
    organization for a presentation, 9–10
    sample for formal oral presentation, 9–10, 85
    slide or poster panel to provide overview of presentation, 9–10
Overview. *See* Outline

P

Pause. *See* Vocalization
Photographs
    providing size scale, 22
    when to use and not use, 20
Pointer. *See* Laser pointer; mechanical pointer
Poster board. *See* Poster presentation
Poster panels
    choice of font for, 30, 56
    choosing template for, 32
    color scheme for, 56
    designing, 56–57

Index **93**

layout, 56
numbering, 32–33, 57
posting, 55–56, 61
title layout on, 57
Poster presentation
allowable space for posting, 56, 58
color scheme for poster panels. *See* Poster panels
controlling distribution of audience. *See* Mechanical pointer
courtesy considerations. *See* Courtesy
criteria for judging in competition, 73
critiquing. *See* Critiquing
developing your own style. *See* Style
digital recording of. *See* On-line materials
distinguishing features of, 53–54
eating and drinking during. *See* Courtesy
engaging audience. *See* Generating interest
example of. *See* On-line materials
extended discussion during, 3, 53–54
eye contact. *See* Eye contact
gimmicks for enhancing. *See* Gimmicks
handling questions, 63, 66–67
having bottle of water for, 60
height to post poster, 61
interacting with audience, 54–55, 63–64
judging criteria for competition, 73
laying out panels. *See* Poster panels
making corrections to, 57–58, 60
mastering mechanics of giving, 63–65
poster board, 53, 55, 58, 61, 65
poster panels. *See* Poster panels
poster sheets, 53, 55–61
preparation before. *See* Preparation
preparation on-site, 60
preparing poster panels. *See* Poster panels
printing, 57–59
printing as individual panels, 55, 57–58
printing as one or more sheets, 57–58
prior studies. *See* Prior studies
proofreading poster panels, 57
proofreading printed poster, 59
recognizing people arriving, 64, 66, 87
recognizing people leaving, 66–67, 87
technical papers competition, 3
time for overview, 63
time required to prepare, 55–57
using banner for title and authors, 57
using mechanical pointer. *See* Mechanical pointer
what to bring, 60–61, 64–66

Poster sheets. *See* Poster presentation
PowerPoint
alternative utilities, 29, 58
inserting slide numbers, 32–33, 56
presentation, 9–10, 27, 29
presentation example of. *See* On-line materials
use of animation, 18, 20, 29–33, 43
use of template, 32
using fade-in, 29, 31–32
using zoom utility, 31–32
Preparation
dressing for the occasion. *See* Dressing for the occasion
on-site, checklist before arriving, 33–35, 60
scoping out facilities, 33–35
scoping out the room, 33–34, 60–61
well in advance of your presentation, 7
Presentation
critiquing. *See* Critiquing
delivery. *See* Style
formal oral. *See* Formal oral presentation
job interview, 3, 11, 18, 24, 34
major components of, 3, 15–16, 24–25
poster. *See* Poster presentation
preparation in advance of. *See* Preparation
previewing slides. *See* Slides
research group meeting, 3, 8, 24, 39, 50
of results, 74
of results showing replicability, 22–23
of results showing reproducibility, 22–23
seminar, 3, 34–35
storing on thumb drive, 34, 59
style. *See* Style
style expression of your personality. *See* Style
technical focus of, 1, 19, 75
technical meeting, 18, 24, 34–35, 50
technical papers competition, 3–4, 11, 73–74
thesis defense, 3, 24
Printing poster. *See* Poster presentation
Prior studies
formats for summarizing, 19
organization of, 19
what to include, 19
Projectors
digital light processor (DLP), 27–28, 30, 41, 53
liquid-crystal display (LCD), 27–28, 30, 41, 53

Proofreading
  not trusting spell and grammar check utilities, 33, 57
  printed poster. See Poster presentation
  slides. See Slides
  by someone whose first language is English, 33, 57

Q

Questions
  answering briefly, 47, 53–54
  avoiding arguments with questioners, 47
  format for recognizing questioners, 47, 66
  handling those you cannot answer, 47
  repeating for audience, 66
  strategy for answering, 47
  thanking and complimenting questioner, 47, 66
Quick reference guides
  formal oral presentation, 69
  poster presentation, 71
Quips
  injecting to handle mistakes, 41
  injecting to handle momentary memory lapse, 42
Quotations. See Quotes
Quotes
  creating electronic file of, 41, 45
  use of, 45, 63, 80

R

Research plan
  for an experimental study, 19–20
  handling equations. See Equations
  including block diagram to indicate solution strategy, 21–22
  indicating design considerations, 19–20
  indicating how problem will be addressed, 17, 19–20, 76
  organization of, 19–21
  providing overview of design and methodology, 21–22
  summarizing assumptions in modeling, 21–22
  summarizing design parameters and range of variables, 20
  summarizing procedure, 20
  for a theoretical study, 19–21
  use of animations to show apparatus, 20, 32, 85
  what to include, 19–21

Results
  discussion of, 22–23
  emphasizing interesting, 23
  formats for presenting, 22
  showing measure of reproducibility of data, 22–23
  showing typical results, 22
Rhetorical question. See Style
Room. See Venue

S

Slides. See also Formal oral presentation
  advancing, 34–36
  avoiding complexity, 29
  changing font color, size, or type for emphasis. See Font
  choice of a template for, 32
  choice of font color. See Font
  choice of font size. See Font
  choice of font type. See Font
  color scheme for formal oral presentation, 30–31
  controlling during presentation, 34–36
  loading before presentation, 34
  numbering, 18, 32–33, 56
  organizing, 17–25
  preliminary considerations, 28–29
  previewing, 34–35
  proofreading, 33, 57–59
  provocative images, 45
  terminology for describing, 28–29
  use of template. See Template
  using animation. See Animation
  using fade-in. See Animation
Sounds
  use of, 32
Style
  avoiding awkward mannerisms, 36, 40
  body language during formal oral presentation, 35–36, 40, 50
  body language during poster presentation, 64
  delivery, 2, 27–28, 51, 54–55, 67
  developing your own, 28, 51, 54–55, 67
  digitally recording to improve, 40, 50–51
  eye contact. See Eye contact
  handling memory lapse. See Memory lapse
  moving around, 39, 64
  posture, 40, 77
  reverse-engineering a talk to improve, 51, 67, 75

suggestions for developing your own, 2, 28, 51, 54–55, 67
use of hands, 36, 40, 64
use of humor. *See* Humor
use of the pause. *See* Vocalization
use of the rhetorical question, 37, 44, 77, 80–83
vocalization. *See* Vocalization
voice inflection. *See* Vocalization
ways to improve, 51, 67

T

Technical challenges. *See* Introduction
Technical papers competitions
  judging criteria, 00018#APP3
  special considerations, 54, 63, 65, 73–74
Templates
  considerations in using, 32
  for poster panels. *See* Poster panels
  for slides. *See* Slides
Thank You slide
  content, 24–25
  including email address, 18, 24–25, 46–47, 76, 86
  reason for using, 24–25
Time
  allocating for each part of presentation, 45–46
  allotted for a formal oral presentation, 9, 28
  allotted for questions after formal oral presentation, 9
  awareness during your presentation, 9, 45–46
  benchmark for reaching your objectives, 45–46
  recommended for each slide, 45–46
  recommended for giving overview of your poster, 63
  warning light system used by some organizations, 46
Title
  considerations, 17–18, 57
  format for listing coauthors, 17–18, 57
  importance of having an effective, 18

introducing numbering of slides, 18
multicultural cultural considerations, 17–18
optional information it can include, 18
strategy for preparing, 17–18
what it must include, 17–18

V

Venue
  contacting session chair to ascertain, 8–9, 33–34, 60–61
  importance of knowing in preparing slides and poster panels, 8–9
  room capacity, 8–9, 33–34
  room geometry, 33–34
  room lighting conditions, 30, 33, 36, 56
  room visiting prior to presentation, 8–9, 33–34, 60–61
  space allocated for your poster, 56
  the site, 8, 34–35, 60–61
Video recording
  of formal oral presentation. *See* On-line materials
  of outstanding speakers. *See* On-line materials
  of poster presentation. *See* On-line materials
Vocalization
  accent handling, 37–38, 48
  avoiding monotone speaking, 37, 77
  considerations, 36–38
  directing question to audience at beginning, 37, 44
  during poster presentation, 67
  multicultural considerations, 37–38, 48
  projecting voice for women, 37
  use of rhetorical question. *See* Style
  use of the pause, 37
  use of the whisper, 37–38
  use of voice inflection, 37
  using microphone. *See* Microphone
  when first language is not English, 37–38, 48
Voice inflection. *See* Vocalization

www.ingramcontent.com/pod-product-compliance
Lightning Source LLC
Chambersburg PA
CBHW071408290426
44108CB00014B/1732